ANNUAL UPDATE

C000016314

US POLITICS

Anthony J. Bennett and Sarra Jenkins

HODDER
EDUCATION
AN HACHETTE UK COMPANY

Acknowledgements

Every effort has been made to trace all copyright holders, but if any have been inadvertently overlooked, the Publishers will be pleased to make the necessary arrangements at the first opportunity.

Although every effort has been made to ensure that website addresses are correct at time of going to press, Hodder Education cannot be held responsible for the content of any website mentioned in this book. It is sometimes possible to find a relocated web page by typing in the address of the home page for a website in the URL window of your browser.

Hachette UK's policy is to use papers that are natural, renewable and recyclable products and made from wood grown in well-managed forests and other controlled sources. The logging and manufacturing processes are expected to conform to the environmental regulations of the country of origin.

Orders: please contact Bookpoint Ltd, 130 Park Drive, Milton Park, Abingdon, Oxon OX14 4SE. Telephone: +44 (0)1235 827827. Fax: +44 (0)1235 400401. E-mail: education@bookpoint.co.uk Lines are open from 9 a.m. to 5 p.m., Monday to Saturday, with a 24-hour message answering service. You can also order through our website: www.hoddereducation.co.uk

ISBN: 978 1 5104 7322 5

© Anthony J. Bennett and Sarra Jenkins 2020

First published in 2020 by

Hodder Education,
An Hachette UK Company
Carmelite House
50 Victoria Embankment
London EC4Y 0DZ

www.hoddereducation.co.uk

Impression number   10 9 8 7 6 5 4 3 2 1

Year   2024 2023 2022 2021 2020

Cover photo © Adobe Stock

Typeset in India

Printed by CPI Group (UK) Ltd, Croydon, CR0 4YY

A catalogue record for this title is available from the British Library.

Contents

Chapter 1

The 2020 presidential election: who is running, what has changed?

Exam success

Presidential elections are a staple topic in the US specification. It is crucial that students are able to make a clear delineation between presidential elections and congressional elections, while understanding similar elements between them. For success in both types of election, it is necessary to win primaries and caucuses and to obtain substantial campaign finance, but the Electoral College exists only in presidential elections. The best students will not only recognise the strengths and weaknesses of this electoral system, but also be able to put it into the current context — for instance, the fact that two of the last five results did not reflect the popular vote, and the role of incumbency especially in the case of 2020. Students must be wary of casting moral judgements on the presidency of Donald Trump — while in many ways he is unique, in others, he is utilising the tools of his office. When judging Trump and the 2020 elections, we must always make our judgements as political scientists!

This topic also has important connections with other topics. The best students will be able to draw from election results the impact they can have on the strength of the presidential mandate and how this can affect a president's relationship with Congress. Similarly, primaries and caucuses can have a damaging effect on party politics and often provide useful insights into the factions within parties. The coat-tails effect during a presidential election year can impact the outcome of congressional elections, which in turn can affect presidential power, depending on whether government is divided or united.

| AQA | 3.2.1.5 | The electoral process |
| Edexcel | 5.1 | Electoral systems in the US |

Context

Presidential elections are held every 4 years, in years divisible by 4: 2012, 2016, 2020, etc. This is set by the Constitution. Federal law determines that the election will be held on the Tuesday after the first Monday in November. In 2020, election day will be Tuesday 3 November. But before the general election campaign between the Democratic and Republican Party candidates can begin, each party's candidate needs to be selected and this is done in a two-stage process: first, through primaries and caucuses; then through the national party conventions. And even before all that occurs, there is what we call 'the invisible primary' when would-be candidates try to position themselves ready for the nomination races by seeking higher name recognition, raising money and getting their organisation in place. Each time this cycle comes round — every 4 years — tweaks are made in the system of selecting the candidates. In this chapter, you will read about: the invisible primary; the likely candidates; the changes made in the system by the two parties; plans already in place for each party's national convention; and some possible changes in the way the Electoral College will elect the president.

The incumbent president

The first thing to ask as we set off on a new presidential election is whether or not the incumbent president is eligible to run for re-election. The Twenty-Second Amendment to the Constitution, passed in 1951, forbade a president from serving more than two terms in office. That is why President Barack Obama could not run again in 2016. He had already been elected twice (2008 and 2012) and had completed his two full terms. But having been first elected in 2016, President Donald Trump is eligible for re-election in 2020 and therefore — barring any unforeseen accident — he will be the Republican Party presidential nominee. How can we be so certain?

- It is almost unheard of for a sitting president to be denied the nomination of his party for a second term. It certainly hasn't happened in the last 50 years.
- Although President Trump has generally low approval ratings (around 45%) among voters in general, he enjoys unusually high approval ratings among likely Republican voters. In July 2019, he enjoyed 90% approval among Republican identifiers.
- It would therefore be extremely hard for any other Republican candidate to gain a significant level of support running against him in the Republican primaries in 2020.

At the time of writing, two Republicans are challenging President Trump for the party's presidential nomination. The first to declare was the former governor of Massachusetts, Bill Weld. Weld will challenge the President from the left of the party. He was followed by one-term congressman Joe Walsh of Illinois, from the party's conservative wing. But neither could be called a 'big name' challenge to the President. Had someone like Mitt Romney or Jeb Bush stepped forward, then they might have been able to mount a serious challenge.

So what will happen in the 2020 Republican nomination race? Most states will still hold their traditional primaries or caucuses between January and June. That said, some states such as South Carolina and Virginia decided early on to cancel their presidential primaries. For example, on 7 September 2019, the Executive Committee of the South Carolina Republican Party voted unanimously to cancel

their party's presidential primary, stating 'there was no rationale to hold a primary' because the incumbent president was running for re-election. In those states that do hold a contest, Trump will probably hoover up 80–90% of the votes and the convention delegates. Turnout is likely to be low. That means we're expecting all the focus to be on the Democrats.

The challengers

Having lost the White House in the 2016 election, the Democrats are the challengers in 2020. And, true to form, the challenging party has collected a long list of would-be candidates. By the middle of 2019, the Democrats had 23 declared presidential candidates (see Table 1.1), more than in any previous election cycle for either party. Two more candidates would join the race in November. With such a large field, we need to divide the candidates into three groups: three front-runners (Biden, Sanders and Warren); two potential dark horses (Buttigieg and Bloomberg); and a host of also-rans. It would be a genuine upset if none of the leading six candidates were eventually to win the nomination. Indeed, many candidates will probably drop out even before a single vote is cast. Twelve candidates had dropped out months before the first votes were to be cast in Iowa.

Table 1.1 Democratic presidential candidates, 2020, in order of entry, showing most recent elective office (dates in 2019 unless stated otherwise)

Candidate	State	Entered race	Left race
Rep. John Delaney	Maryland	28 July 2017	
Andrew Yang	New York	6 November 2017	
Rep. Tulsi Gabbard	Hawaii	11 January	
*Mayor Julián Castro	Texas	12 January	
Senator Kamala Harris	California	21 January	(12) 3 December
Senator Cory Booker	New Jersey	1 February	
Senator Elizabeth Warren	Massachusetts	9 February	
Senator Amy Klobuchar	Minnesota	10 February	
Senator Bernie Sanders	Vermont	19 February	
*Governor Jay Inslee	Washington	1 March	(3) 21 August
*Governor John Hickenlooper	Colorado	4 March	(2) 15 August
*Rep. Beto O'Rourke	Texas	14 March	(8) 1 November
Senator Kirsten Gillibrand	New York	17 March	(5) 28 August
Mayor Wayne Messam	Florida	28 March	(9) 19 November
Rep. Tim Ryan	Ohio	4 April	(7) 24 October
Rep. Eric Swalwell	California	8 April	(1) 8 July
Mayor Pete Buttigieg	Indiana	14 April	

Candidate	State	Entered race	Left race
Rep. Seth Moulton	Massachusetts	22 April	(4) 23 August
*Vice President Joe Biden	Delaware	25 April	
Senator Michael Bennet	Colorado	2 May	
Governor Steve Bullock	Montana	14 May	(11) 2 December
Mayor Bill de Blasio	New York	16 May	(6) 20 September
*Rep. Joe Sestak	Pennsylvania	23 June	(10) 1 December
*Governor Deval Patrick	Massachusetts	14 November	
*Mayor Michael Bloomberg	New York	21 November	

* = not an incumbent

Table 1.1 also shows a much wider pool of recruitment than that from which presidential candidates are usually drawn. Of course, one needs to keep in mind that Donald Trump won both his party's presidential nomination and the general election in 2016 having held no political office at all. But the most common pools of recruitment for the White House are the vice presidency, state governorships and the Senate. Of Trump's ten immediate predecessors – from JFK to Obama – four came from the vice presidency, four from state governorships and two from the Senate. Yet only 12 of these 25 candidates (48%) come from these three pools – seven from the Senate, four state governors and one former vice president. The big surprise is that for seven of them their most recent political office was to serve as a member of the House of Representatives. No one has ever been elected to the presidency directly from the House. And the same is true of city mayors, yet five mayors – either serving or former – were in the 2020 field for the Democrats. Many of these seemed closely to resemble some of the so-called 'vanity candidates' who contested the UK Conservative Party leadership election in the summer of 2019.

So why do no-hopers run? Well, some of them might indeed fall under the unenviable umbrella of 'vanity candidates' – having inflated opinions of their own abilities. Others might be putting down a marker for 2024 or even beyond, while still others might hope to be offered either the vice presidential slot on the ticket, or maybe a cabinet post in any future Democratic administration. After the 2016 election, two of Donald Trump's Republican primary opponents landed a seat in the cabinet – Ben Carson (Housing and Urban Development) and Rick Perry (Energy).

Some of these candidates will drop out before the voting in the primaries and caucuses even starts. They lack the impetus, the poll numbers, the media exposure and the money to keep going. Indeed, by December 2019, twelve candidates had

ended their campaigns (see the right-hand column of Table 1.1). Some may run for other offices in 2020; others may wait and hope for a call to be the eventual candidate's running-mate; some will doubtless reappear in 2024 or 2028.

As the Democratic primaries and caucuses run their course through the first half of 2020, there are three questions you can ask to help you analyse the direction in which the Democrats seem to be moving as they prepare for the November elections:

1 Is the party breaking new ground with its nomination or keeping to the tried and tested paths of previous elections? If the Democrats are looking backwards, then expect Biden to be running away with the race. He is a 77-year-old, white, male candidate who was first elected to the Senate in 1972 where he served for 36 years before serving as President Obama's vice president for a further 8 years. Biden is Mr Continuity. If the Democrats are really breaking new ground, then they will turn to someone like Cory Booker or Pete Buttigieg.

2 Is the party aiming for the middle ground with Clinton-type policies, or is it moving significantly to the left? If it is the former, then Biden is well placed. But if the party is looking to move to the left, then Sanders and Warren should be doing well.

3 How much importance are Democratic voters giving to electability? In a significant *ABC News/Washington Post* poll in early July 2019, Trump was in a tie with Warren and Buttigieg, in a statistical dead heat with Sanders and Harris, but trailed Biden by 10 percentage points. How much will head-to-head polls like this be weighing on the minds of Democrat voters as they vote in their primaries and caucuses?

The Democratic primaries

Table 1.2 shows the Democratic Party's nomination calendar for 2020 with the contest expected to kick off, as is traditional, in Iowa — on 3 February — and then to run for 4 months before wrapping up on 2 June.

Table 1.2 Democratic Party nomination calendar

Date	State	Type*	Delegates
3 February	Iowa	Caucuses	49
11 February	New Hampshire	Modified primary	33
22 February	Nevada	Caucuses	48
29 February	South Carolina	Open primary	63

Date	State	Type*	Delegates
3 March (Super Tuesday)	Alabama	Open primary	61
	Arkansas	Open primary	36
	California	Modified primary	495
	Colorado	Modified primary	80
	Maine	Closed primary	32
	Massachusetts	Modified primary	114
	Minnesota	Closed primary	92
	North Carolina	Modified primary	122
	Oklahoma	Modified primary	42
	Tennessee	Open primary	73
	Texas	Closed primary	262
	Utah	Closed primary	35
	Vermont	Open primary	23
	Virginia	Open primary	124
10 March	Idaho	Closed primary	25
	Michigan	Open primary	147
	Mississippi	Open primary	41
	Missouri	Open primary	78
	North Dakota	Open primary	18
	Washington	Closed primary	107
17 March	Arizona	Closed primary	78
	Florida	Closed primary	248
	Illinois	Open primary	184
	Ohio	Modified primary	153
24 March	Georgia	Open primary	120
4 April	Alaska	Closed primary	18
	Hawaii	Closed primary	31
	Louisiana	Closed primary	57
	Wyoming	Caucuses	17
7 April	Wisconsin	Open primary	90
28 April	Connecticut	Closed primary	64
	Delaware	Closed primary	28
	Maryland	Closed primary	102
	New York	Closed primary	270
	Pennsylvania	Closed primary	176
	Rhode Island	Modified primary	30
2 May	Kansas	Closed primary	39
5 May	Indiana	Open primary	72

Date	State	Type*	Delegates
12 May	Nebraska	Modified primary	29
	West Virginia	Modified primary	30
19 May	Kentucky	Closed primary	52
	Oregon	Closed primary	66
2 June	Montana	Open primary	22
	New Jersey	Modified primary	128
	New Mexico	Closed primary	40
	South Dakota	Modified primary	19
	Washington DC	Closed primary	43

* See Box 1.1 for information about the types of primary.

Box 1.1　Types of primary

Open primary: a primary in which any registered voter can vote in either party's primary.

Closed primary: a primary in which only registered Democrats can vote in a Democratic primary and only registered Republicans can vote in a Republican primary.

Modified primary: like a closed primary, in that only registered party voters can vote, but it also allows those who have registered as independents to vote in either party's primary.

Three significant changes

Super Tuesday

Three significant changes have occurred in the Democrats' nomination calendar and process since 2016. The first is that Super Tuesday — traditionally the first Tuesday in March — is even more 'super' than it was 4 years ago. In 2016, 11 states held their contests on that day. Now, in 2020, there will be 14 state contests — including California, which has moved its primary from the first Monday of March in 2016. That means that five of the largest state delegations will be chosen on 3 March 2020 — California (495), Texas (262), Virginia (124), North Carolina (122) and Massachusetts (114).

'Fairly super' Tuesday

The second significant change is that on the second Tuesday in March, there will be a 'fairly super Tuesday' event with six states holding their primaries on that day. In 2016, only two states voted in the week after Super Tuesday. This 'fairly super' Tuesday sees another two large state delegations chosen — in Michigan (147) and Washington (107). So altogether on those first two Tuesdays in March, 20 states will vote in the Democratic primaries. That means that by that time, almost half the states (24) will already have voted. And by the end of March, 68% of all the delegates to the Democratic national party convention will have been chosen (see Figure 1.1). That is what we call 'front loading' — when half the states cram their contests into the first 5 weeks of the calendar, with still almost 3 months to go. The British poet T. S. Eliot (1888–1965) wrote that 'April is the cruellest month', but for many Democratic presidential candidates in 2020, it could very well turn out to be March!

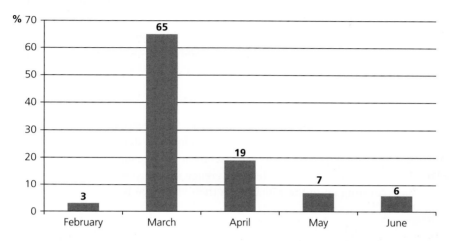

Figure 1.1 Percentage of Democratic Party national convention delegates chosen per month, 2020

Fewer caucuses

The third significant change is a change not in the calendar but in the process itself. In last year's *US Update* we covered the proposals of the grandly named Unity Reform Commission (URC) set up by the Democratic Party 'to study and address concerns that arose regarding the presidential nominating process' in 2016. The commission was tasked with 'ensuring that the process is accessible, transparent and inclusive'. One thing it was particularly concerned with was the use of caucuses in many states. As we pointed out last year, the trouble with caucuses is that they attract an even smaller and more unrepresentative group of voters than primaries. Caucuses — which are meetings held across the state — attract the more politically and ideologically committed. They also discourage participation among those who cannot, for reasons of work, infirmity, disability, age or family commitments, attend the meeting. Whereas in a primary, one merely has to call into the voting station for a few minutes at any time during a (usually) 10–11-hour opening time, caucuses are held in the evening and often last for 2 or 3 hours. The URC report therefore stated:

> At a time when voting rights are under attack… many are concerned that cau-
> cuses disenfranchise voters, such as seniors, members of the military, working
> families, students, and parents of young children, who are not able to attend
> a caucus meeting or spend hours while internal meeting processes continue
> in order to exercise their right to participate in the presidential nominating
> process.

The commission therefore instructed its state parties that use caucuses to 'find new and better ways to ensure broad participation'.

Often these party commissions have little lasting effect on the process. But it seems that, at least in this respect, the URC may be an exception. For 2020 will see a very significant decline in the use of caucuses in the Democrats' presidential nominating process. Whereas in 2016, 14 states held Democratic caucuses rather than primaries, in 2020 that figure is likely to fall to just three. Among the states switching from caucuses to a primary for the Democrats are Colorado, Minnesota and Washington. The three state Democratic parties sticking with caucuses are Iowa, Nevada and Wyoming.

But no 'virtual' caucuses

In two of these three states — Iowa and Nevada — the Democrats had tried to make them more accessible to would-be voters. The plan was that registered Democrats in these states who would be unable to attend the party caucuses on the stated day would be able to participate in a teleconference or internet-based Virtual Caucus in the days running up to the caucuses in their state (see Box 1.2).

> ### Box 1.2 Proposed Iowa Democratic Party Virtual Caucus dates and times
>
> - Wednesday, 29 January at 7 p.m. (local time)
> - Thursday, 30 January at 12 noon
> - Friday, 31 January at 7.30 a.m.
> - Saturday, 1 February at 10 a.m.
> - Sunday, 2 February at 2 p.m.
> - Monday, 3 February at 7 p.m.

The range of different times over six days was clearly meant to encourage participation by voters unwilling or unable to attend a lengthy evening meeting often miles from their home because of, for example, work or child care commitments, ill-health or disability. But in late August 2019, the Democratic National Committee (DNC) scuppered these initiatives because of cyber-security concerns. At a closed-door session of the DNC's Rules and By-Laws Committee, it was revealed that experts commissioned by the party had been able to hack into a conference call between the committee, the Iowa Democratic Party and the Nevada Democratic Party, raising concerns about teleconferencing for virtual caucuses. Within a week, the DNC announced that it was banning the planned virtual caucuses for the 2020 election cycle.

The DNC's decision was sharply criticised by a number of the party's 'lower order' presidential candidates, who had hoped that the likely broader and increased turnout would have benefited their campaigns. 'It's important if we're going to win this election against Donald Trump in 2020 that you get people off the sidelines,' said one such candidate, Julián Castro, following the DNC announcement. 'And you ain't going to get them off the sidelines if you promise people that you're going to have more opportunity to get out and vote and now go back on your word.' No one sees any quick fix for this, and with election security still a prime concern, don't expect any more movement on this in the near future.

Electability

The Democrats are desperate to win in 2020, if only to avenge their non-defeat in 2016. As we shall discuss later in this chapter, the Democrats won the popular vote in 2016 by almost 3 million votes but lost the election in the Electoral College. The post mortems in 2016 suggested that their choice of candidate — Hillary Clinton — had been unwise because she is such a polarising character. Furthermore, suggestions were made that Clinton's campaign was not well run and that both she and her staff were too complacent. Specifically, it was said that they thought certain states such as Michigan, Pennsylvania and Wisconsin were in the bag, only to lose all three by a whisker on Election Day.

So although policies will feature highly in the Democratic primaries, what Democrats really want is to pick a winner. Keep an eye on the head-to-head polls in which President Trump is pitched against different Democratic front-runners — Biden, Sanders, Warren and the like. In a *Washington Post/ABC News* poll conducted in mid-September 2019, likely Democratic voters believed that Biden was far and away their most electable candidate (see Figure 1.2). When these candidates were pitched against President Trump, all came out ahead of the President — Biden by 16 percentage points (38–54%), Sanders by 12 points (40–52%) and Warren by 11 points (40–51%).[1]

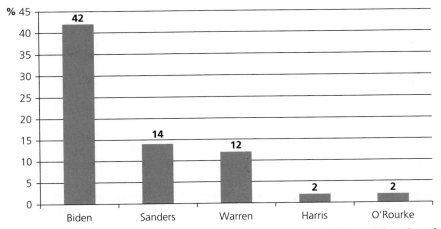

Figure 1.2 Percentage of Democrat-leaning voters who think the candidate has the best chance of defeating President Trump

Source: *Washington Post/ABC News* poll, September 2019

---

1 You can keep an eye on how these and other polls are shaping up during 2020 by visiting www.realclearpolitics.com.

National party conventions

Being the challenging party, the Democrats will go first with their national convention. This will be held on 13–16 July in Milwaukee, Wisconsin — the first time the city has ever hosted a national convention of any party. The Republicans have scheduled their national convention on 24–27 August in Charlotte, North Carolina. The city hosted the Democratic convention in 2012 but has never before hosted the Republicans. It is significant that both parties have chosen key battleground states in which to hold their respective conventions. In 2016, the Democrats lost Wisconsin in the general election by just 23,000 votes out of nearly 3 million votes cast state-wide. North Carolina is a key state for the Republicans to hold in a Trump re-election bid; they won it in 2016 by fewer than 200,000 votes out of the nearly 5 million cast.

The Democrats have made another significant rule change for their convention in 2020. Of the expected 4,534 delegates to be chosen, 3,769 will be chosen in the primaries and will be committed to vote for the candidates for whom they were elected in the primaries. The remaining 765 delegates are the ex officio super-delegates — professional politicians such as senators, House members, governors, big city mayors, members of the state and national party committees — who are chosen as uncommitted delegates and can vote how they please at the convention.

But the super-delegates caused controversy at the 2016 Democratic convention. For whereas among the committed delegates chosen in the primaries, Hillary Clinton held a narrow lead — 54% to 46% — over her chief rival Bernie Sanders, the super-delegates broke 93% for Clinton and just 7% for Sanders, thereby guaranteeing Clinton the nomination on the first ballot at the convention.

The big change for 2020 is that super-delegates will no longer be eligible to vote in the first ballot unless there is absolutely no doubt about the outcome. This would be the case if one candidate had already gained an absolute majority of the committed delegates (1,885) chosen in the primaries and caucuses. If no candidate wins an absolute majority on the first ballot, then all delegates become 'uncommitted' and the super-delegates will be permitted to participate in all subsequent ballots.

What is the significance of all this? It increases the democratic accountability of the convention, ensuring that, at least on the first ballot, the will of the voters in the primaries and caucuses is respected. The Republicans don't have super-delegates, so there are no changes in their convention procedures in 2020.

The Electoral College

Yet another thing that might change in the 2020 presidential election is the way the Electoral College works (see Box 1.3). There is something of a pattern developing here, for just as the changes in the Democratic Party's primaries and caucuses were meant to make the process more democratic and more accountable, so the changes some states are proposing in the Electoral College have the same aim in mind.

The background to this is the result of the 2016 presidential election when the Electoral College elected the candidate who had come second in the popular vote (see Table 1.3).

- Despite Hillary Clinton (D) beating Donald Trump by over 2 percentage points (almost 3 million votes) in the popular vote, Trump won by 304 votes to 227 in the Electoral College.
- The same thing had happened in 2000, leading to the election of George W. Bush, although on that occasion the popular vote margin between the two candidates was much smaller — only half-a-million votes.
- The 2016 result occurred because of the winner-take-all rule that most (48) states use for allocating their Electoral College votes.
- Donald Trump won four states — with a total of 75 Electoral College votes — by the thinnest of margins (see Table 1.3). In these states, Clinton lost overall by fewer than 200,000 votes, out of over 22 million, yet in the Electoral College Trump won 75 votes and Clinton received none.
- At the same time, Clinton was winning her large states by huge margins — California (29 percentage points), Illinois (16 points), Massachusetts (27 points) and New York (22 points) — thereby racking up millions of 'wasted votes' in these states.

To try to prevent this phenomenon from occurring again in 2020, a number of states have been signing up to the National Popular Vote Interstate Compact (NPVIC). As mentioned above, 48 states currently use a state-based, winner-take-all system by which all of the state's Electoral College votes are awarded to whichever candidate wins the popular vote in that state. All states bar Nebraska and Maine use this system, and you can see the effect it has in Table 1.4. In Michigan in 2016, although Hillary Clinton polled only 10,704 votes fewer than Donald Trump — out of over 4.5 million — she won no Electoral College votes. Trump won all of Michigan's 16 electoral votes.

Table 1.3 Popular and Electoral College votes compared: selected states

State	Donald Trump (R)		Hillary Clinton (D)	
	Popular vote	ECV	Popular vote	ECV
Florida	4,617,886	29	4,504,975	0
Michigan	2,279,543	16	2,268,839	0
Pennsylvania	2,970,733	20	2,926,441	0
Wisconsin	1,405,284	10	1,382,536	0
Total	11,273,446	75	11,082,791	0

Table 1.4 Popular and Electoral College votes, 2016

Candidate	Popular vote (%)	Electoral College votes
Hillary Clinton (D)	48.2	227
Donald Trump (R)	46.1	304

The NPVIC is an agreement among a group of states to award all their Electoral College votes to the winner of the *national* popular vote. In other words, had this been in operation in 2016, all participating states would have cast all their electoral votes for Hillary Clinton regardless of who won the popular vote in their state. At the time of writing, 15 states plus the District of Columbia had signed up to this compact. Between them, they control 196 electoral votes. That is important, because the compact has legal force only if it is signed up to by states controlling at least 270 Electoral College votes — that being the number a candidate needs to win the presidency.

States already signed up to the compact include California, New York, Illinois and New Jersey. Efforts to sign up states to the compact have already failed in eight states, including Nevada where the legislation, having passed both houses of the state legislature, was vetoed by Governor Steve Sisolak in May 2019. Legislation to join the compact was pending (at the time of writing) in nine states commanding a further 108 electoral votes. But in only one of those nine states — Minnesota — has the relevant legislation been introduced into both houses of the state legislature, and even in Minnesota the bill has reached no further than the committee stage. Overall, therefore, this change looks unlikely to come into effect — at least not for 2020.

One postscript. When you see or hear President Trump making remarks — either in tweets or at rallies — disparaging American people of colour (remember 'Send Her Back!' in July 2019?), what the President is hoping to achieve is to drive up the turnout of non-college-educated white voters in states like Michigan, Pennsylvania and Wisconsin, so that even if he loses the popular vote across the nation by as big a margin — or by an even bigger margin — than in 2016, he will still be able to eke out a win in the Electoral College. That is his strategy.

Comparison

While both the USA and UK use the first-past-the-post electoral system at national level, the methods of selecting candidates to run in these elections are very different:

■ The primary system in the USA theoretically allows for wider representation of different groups, who can all put themselves forward as candidates. By comparison, in the UK party control over local shortlists means the public has limited choice over candidate selection. The Conservatives did experiment with a system similar to primaries leading to the selection and election of Sarah Woolaston MP, but this has not been used since.

■ The use of first-past-the-post can explain the dominance of two parties in both countries. While the UK has arguably seen an increase in the number of parties winning seats in recent years, it remains the case that in both the USA and the UK, only two parties are likely to win enough seats to gain a majority at national level.

■ Both the USA and UK have people who are chosen by indirect election. In the USA, the president is indirectly elected through the Electoral College, while in the UK the prime minister is the leader of the party that forms the government, not someone who is directly elected by the British electorate. This is especially obvious when considering that 17 times since 1900 the office of prime minister has been held by someone who did not 'win' that role by leading their party in an election.

Summary

In this chapter, we have covered the following issues:

■ Incumbency — the position of a sitting president in a re-election year. We saw that the Constitution limits a president to two full terms in office. We also saw that an incumbent president is nearly always guaranteed the nomination of his party for a second term.

■ The most likely pools of recruitment from which presidential candidates are drawn.

■ The open nature of the nomination process — in terms of the number and range of candidates who compete, and the steps taken to encourage voter participation in the nomination procession. This makes the process for selecting presidential candidates in the USA far more open and participatory than what we saw for the election of a new prime minister in the UK in 2019.

■ The importance of the nomination calendar. Front loading benefits well-known and well-financed candidates over insurgents.

■ The restricting of the power of the Democrats' super-delegates — another attempt to make their nomination process more accountable and democratic.

■ The importance of electability for the Democrats in 2020.

■ Attempts by some states to prevent the popular vote loser from being declared the winner in the Electoral College, as occurred in both 2000 and 2016.

You should therefore look to use the information in this chapter to strengthen your arguments regarding the open, participatory and democratic nature of the US presidential nomination process, especially within the Democratic Party.

Further reading and research

- To follow the presidential primary results as they are announced from February 2020, use the following websites:
  www.washingtonpost.com
  www.nytimes.com
  www.thegreenpapers.com/G20
- For the latest polls — both for the Democratic nomination race and for possible general election head-to-head polling — see:
  www.realclearpolitics.com.
- For more detailed analysis of the nomination race and the general election as it develops, see: www.fivethirtyeight.com.
- On further developments regarding the NPVIC, refer to:
  www.nationalpopularvote.com.

Chapter 2

The Mueller investigation

Exam success

The Mueller investigation (2017–19) is a useful case study for students in trying to determine the extent of presidential power and the checks that exist upon it. It was an investigation of the possible links between the Trump campaign of 2016 and Russia, and of potential obstruction of justice by President Trump, and it was conducted by the Justice Department, not by Congress.

It is crucial to understand this because the Justice Department is contained within the executive branch. The department is one of the 15 executive departments within the federal bureaucracy and is headed by the Attorney General, who is a presidential appointee. This was, therefore, an investigation into the executive by the executive branch. While Mueller later gave evidence in Congress about his investigation, the best students will understand that this is an example, not of constitutional checks and balances, but of other limitations on the president, including his own appointees and the media.

It is an especially useful example for examinations as it speaks to the informal limitations on presidents. As Professor Neustadt argued in 1960, presidential power is often determined by factors far beyond the formal powers given by the Constitution. The president's personality, skills and experience also determine his power. The Mueller investigation provides a rare example of the informal limitations that can be placed upon presidential power by raising issues concerning the president's personality, skills and experience. It also, however, demonstrates the limitations of such an investigation, the conclusions of which were subject to the Justice Department's own rules. It is a complex case study, but the basics should be accessible to all students, while students aiming for the top marks will be able to deploy it on both sides of an argument concerning presidential power, the role of congressional oversight, or the limitations and effectiveness of the US Constitution.

AQA	3.2.1.3	The executive branch of government: president
Edexcel	3.2	Informal sources of presidential power and their use
	3.3	The presidency
	3.4	Interpretations and debates of the US presidency

Context

The Trump administration has experienced a number of unique moments in modern presidential history. The turnover in the executive branch staff, the lowest poll ratings for a president after 100 days and also 1 year, and an unusual approach to social media stand out among a range of other occurrences. The Mueller investigation, launched in May 2017, was in part the result of some of these events.

The Mueller investigation looked into Russian interference in the 2016 US elections and potentially suspicious links between Trump associates and the Russian government. It followed the hacking and release of thousands of emails from the Clinton campaign and the subsequent firing of FBI Director James Comey.

Comey's sacking was the catalyst for a wider investigation into these accusations. Although the Attorney General at the time was Jeff Sessions, he had been involved in the Trump campaign as well as being a key Trump appointee, and he therefore recused (excused) himself. So the Deputy Attorney General appointed Robert Mueller, former FBI Director under Presidents Bush and Obama, to the role of Special Counsel to carry out the investigation. Between May 2017 and March 2019, the investigation looked at two key questions: was there 'collusion' between the Trump campaign and Russian operatives, and was President Trump trying to 'obstruct justice' as the investigation continued? It is important to note that whether Russia interfered in the 2016 election was not up for debate — it had already been determined that it had. For many Democrats, the investigation represented an opportunity to find information from which President Trump could be impeached.

Box 2.1 Key terms

Subpoena — a legal document requiring someone to give evidence, or to provide any requested documents.

Attorney General — the presidential appointee heading the Justice Department, ratified by the Senate.

Special Counsel —a person with the powers of a US attorney, such as to subpoena records, who is appointed to investigate an issue but who is removed from the ordinary chain of command in the Justice Department and who can therefore act with some independence.

Indictment — a formal accusation of wrongdoing, usually resulting in an arrest and formal charges against someone.

Recusal — the withdrawal of someone from an investigation due to a conflict of interest.

The investigation

The Mueller investigation was launched in May 2017. Robert Mueller was appointed as a 'Special Counsel' to head the investigation (see Box 2.1). According to Justice Department regulations, a Special Counsel is to be appointed when an investigation might represent a conflict of interest. As many of the top officials in the Justice Department either worked on the Trump campaign or were appointed by him, appointing Mueller as Special Counsel gave him a level of independence in conducting the investigation and prevented interference from the White House.

Mueller was tasked with looking at whether the Trump presidential campaign of 2016 had either known about or actively worked with Russia in Russia's interference in the election. This interference included the hacking and release of Democratic National Committee emails and using social media 'troll farms' to influence voters to support the Trump campaign rather than Clinton. By June 2017, the investigation had extended to investigating whether President Trump had obstructed justice — whether he and his allies had hidden evidence and tried to manipulate witnesses in order to mislead the investigation. Key to this second issue was trying to work out:

- What did President Trump know about Russian interference?
- What did President Trump and his staff do that might constitute 'colluding' with Russia?
- Did President Trump encourage a cover-up of these actions?

As part of the investigation, Robert Mueller was able to subpoena witnesses and documents. The investigation heard from numerous key players from the Trump campaign (see Box 2.2).

Box 2.2 The key players

Robert Mueller	James Comey	William Barr
Role: Special Counsel to investigate potential links between the Trump campaign in 2016 and Russia. Appointed May 2017, completed report March 2019, resigned June 2019, gave evidence to Congress August 2019.	*Role*: former FBI Director, initiated investigations into the relationship between the Trump campaign and Russia in 2016 after the release on Wikileaks of thousands of Clinton emails; later fired by President Trump.	*Role*: Attorney General replacing Jeff Sessions; issued a four-page summary of the Mueller investigation before pressure forced a full, if redacted, version to be released to Congress.
Jeff Sessions	**Paul Manafort**	**Rick Gates**
Role: former Attorney General. Recused himself from involvement in the investigation, allowing the Deputy Attorney General to appoint Robert Mueller.	*Role*: former Trump campaign chairman. *Outcome*: sentenced to 7½ years in prison for financial crimes.	*Role*: former Trump campaign aide. *Outcome*: pleaded guilty to lying to investigators, then cooperated with them as a witness. Awaiting sentencing.

Michael Cohen	Michael Flynn	Roger Stone
Role: former personal lawyer to President Trump.	*Role*: former Trump National Security Adviser, foreign policy adviser in the Trump campaign.	*Role*: Trump confidant.
Outcome: pleaded guilty to financial crimes, campaign finance violations and lying to Congress. He cooperated with investigators for a lighter sentence. Sentenced to 3 years in prison.	*Outcome*: pleaded guilty to lying to the FBI about conversations with Russian operatives. Mueller recommended no prison time for him.	*Outcome*: indicted for lying to Congress and witness tampering. He was found guilty on charges and is awaiting sentencing.

Trump and the investigation

Many individuals were subpoenaed to give evidence, but the investigation could not reach an agreement with the White House to take oral evidence from President Trump himself, despite trying for over a year. While the Trump administration was happy for him to give evidence regarding Russian interference, it was not happy for Trump to be questioned on obstruction of justice. In the end, the Trump administration agreed to provide only written answers. These answers were deemed to be 'inadequate' and 'incomplete' by investigators, with President Trump saying that he did not recall in his answers more than 30 times. The Trump administration disagreed with this view, arguing that it had provided more than 30 witnesses and 1.4 million pages of evidence.

Box 2.3	The timeline
March 2016	The personal account of John Podesta, the chair of Clinton's presidential campaign, is hacked.
July 2016	The FBI under Director James Comey begins an investigation into possible links between the Trump election campaign and Russia.
October 2016	20,000 pages of Podesta emails are released on Wikileaks.
9 May 2017	FBI Director James Comey is fired by President Trump.
17 May 2017	Robert Mueller is appointed as Special Counsel to lead a Justice Department inquiry into possible 'collusion' between the Trump campaign and Russia, and possible obstruction of justice by President Trump. During the investigation, numerous indictments, plea deals and sentences are handed down to a number of individuals involved in the Trump 2016 campaign (see Box 2.2 for more information).

14 March 2019	The House of Representatives votes 420–0 to make the final Mueller report public. This is blocked by the Republican-controlled Senate.
22 March 2019	The full 448-page Mueller report is delivered to Attorney General Barr and the investigation officially ends.
24 March 2019	Attorney General Barr issues a four-page summary of the Mueller report, saying that it had not uncovered evidence that the Trump campaign had conspired with Russia and that it had drawn no conclusion concerning the obstruction of justice.
18 April 2019	The full report is released with some redactions.
24 July 2019	Robert Mueller appears before two congressional committees, having been subpoenaed.

The report

The report was published in March 2019. In response to the two key questions the investigation, firstly, found that the Trump administration had not criminally conspired to influence the 2016 election with Russian operatives; and secondly, did not find explicitly that the President had *not* tried to obstruct justice. The report stated:

> If we had confidence after a thorough investigation of the facts that the president clearly did not commit obstruction of justice, we would so state.

Alongside this, the report listed ten episodes in which the President had potentially tried to obstruct the investigation (see Box 2.4). However, it also pointed out that Justice Department guidelines meant a sitting president could not be indicted for these, perhaps suggesting that the case could not be made because of President's Trump's office rather than because of a lack of evidence. Certainly the report stated that the President could not be exonerated on this count, saying that if the investigators had believed that President Trump 'clearly did not commit a crime, we would have said so'.

Box 2.4 **Ten situations in which Trump allegedly obstructed justice, identified in the Mueller report**

1 President Trump asking FBI Director Comey to end the investigation into Michael Flynn.
2 President Trump asking White House Counsel McGahn to stop Attorney General Sessions from recusing himself.
3 President Trump firing FBI Director Comey.
4 President Trump's public criticism of Robert Mueller's appointment and the Justice Department, and his attempts to have Mueller removed.
5 President Trump's efforts to stop the investigation by sending messages through his staff asking Attorney General Sessions to end it.
6 President Trump directing aides not to allow investigators to see emails.

7 President Trump asking Attorney General Sessions to undo his recusal from the investigation.

8 President Trump asking White House Counsel McGahn to deny that he had been asked to try to remove Robert Mueller as Special Counsel.

9 President Trump asking Michael Flynn to let him know what information he was going to give to the investigation, and praising Paul Manafort for not cooperating.

10 President Trump's criticism of Michael Cohen when he cooperated with the investigation.

The testimony in Congress

Mueller was subpoenaed to give evidence about his report to the Justice and Intelligence Committees in Congress in July 2019. The hype surrounding his appearance was immense and there were a number of Democrats who clearly believed his testimony might fuel the case for impeachment of President Trump. Before giving evidence, however, Mueller was reminded by the Justice Department that he was bound by their rules and regulations and must stay within the confines of the report when giving evidence.

The result was something of a damp squib. Numerous times throughout the questioning, Mueller's response was 'I can't answer that question', 'that's out of my purview' or 'I'll refer you to the report'. He was asked if the report was a total exoneration of the President, to which he answered, 'no'. The hearings outraged both Democrats and Republicans – Democrats were angry that the President could not be exonerated, saying this was evidence of wrongdoing, while Republicans were angry that the President was being treated as 'below the law', required to prove his own innocence rather than the investigators having to prove his guilt.

Analysis: the impact of the investigation

The investigation gives a number of key takeaways for students. Firstly, it demonstrates both the control and lack thereof that the president has over the executive branch. The closest part of the executive branch to the president is the Executive Office of the President (EXOP), located mostly in the White House or nearby buildings. From the Mueller report, we can see that President Trump clearly felt he was able to control the actions of aides within EXOP. He directed them to withhold evidence, and to ask for the removal of individuals from key positions in the investigation, suggesting significant control over this body.

However, it is also clear that in some aspects the only reason that President Trump did not obstruct justice was because his aides felt uncomfortable with what they were being asked to do, and therefore ignored his directions. White House Counsel McGahn is a clear example of this – President Trump asked him to phone Attorney General Sessions to say that Mueller had a conflict of interest and should be removed. McGahn simply did not carry out this order. In fact, it could be suggested that the only reason why President Trump did not obstruct justice was that his staff either ignored or failed to carry out his orders. It is unusual for such disloyalty to be evident in EXOP, which is shaped to each president's desire. Events therefore demonstrated an unusual lack of control and power on the part of the President; they certainly do not demonstrate him to be in control of his own staff.

The investigation also demonstrates the lack of presidential control over the wider executive branch. Attorney General Sessions was appointed by Trump to head up the Justice Department, and therefore should have owed some loyalty to him. However, President Trump seemed unable to control this member of his cabinet, with Sessions recusing himself from the investigation against Trump's wishes. Nonetheless, Trump did ultimately demonstrate his power over the cabinet, firing Sessions and appointing Barr as his replacement. The same is true of James Comey, fired for his continued investigation into Russian interference against Trump's wishes. Cabinet members traditionally last only 2–3 years, and a president can appoint whomever he likes provided he can get the appointment approved by the Senate.

The fact that Congress pressed for the release of the full report, and that it was congressional anger at the firing of Comey that led to the investigation even beginning, speaks to the ways in which Congress can advance oversight of the executive branch even beyond its constitutional powers. However, each member of the committees that heard testimony from Mueller only had 5 minutes to question him. It could therefore be asked how effective such oversight is when the time limits are so short and the report itself was redacted. The relationship between the president and Congress therefore remains one where the president is proactive and Congress is reactive, acting only when it is often too late to prevent wrongdoing.

The impact of the investigation can also be measured by reviewing the calls for impeachment of President Trump that the Mueller report created. In any impeachment of a president, there must be 218 votes in its favour in the House of Representatives, which then brings about proceedings in the Senate. The impeachment is tried by the Senate and is presided over by the Chief Justice of the Supreme Court. A two-thirds majority vote is required for a president to be found guilty and removed from office. At the time of the Mueller investigation, the Democrats held 235 seats in the House of Representatives, but they did not have enough support to begin impeachment proceedings on the basis of the report alone. However, following the report and Mueller's testimony in Congress, 36 more Democrats did come forward in favour of impeachment, bringing the total in support to over 100. Nonetheless, even if the House of Representatives had managed to find enough support for the motion, there remained a Republican majority in the Senate, which meant the chances of a guilty verdict to impeachment remained, and remains, slim.

It is also noteworthy that a number of congressional investigations related to this report continue into President Trump. The House and Senate Intelligence Committees and the Senate Judiciary Committee are investigating the Russian interference in the 2016 election and possible collusion from the Trump campaign, while the House Oversight Committee is investigating links between President Trump and Russian officials. Such investigations are important symbols of the power that Congress has to hold the President to account. However, if the wide-ranging Mueller investigation failed to find collusion, it seems unlikely that these committees will be able to.

The final impact that the investigation may have is on the 2020 election. So far, the report and testimony in Congress seem to have had limited impact on poll ratings for President Trump. However, some Democratic candidates for president have called for his impeachment in their primary campaigns – Senator Warren, Senator Booker, former Vice President Biden, Mayor Buttigieg, former Secretary Castro, Senator Harris and former Representative O'Rourke. As part of his testimony, Mueller also warned about Russian interference in the 2020 election, saying: 'It wasn't a single attempt. They are doing it while we sit here. And they expect to do it during the next campaign.' He also claimed that Russian interference in the election was one of the greatest threats to US democracy. While the two main parties agree broadly that this is a real threat, they do not agree about how to solve it.

Comparison

In both the USA and the UK, the power of the executive has come under intense scrutiny in recent years:

- Both the US and UK cabinets have seen a vast number of firings and resignations resulting from cabinet members objecting to the policies of their executives. This speaks to a growing similarity in their role despite the stark differences between the expectations of the US and UK cabinets.
- Both the US and UK executives have seen growing challenges to their authority launched by the legislature, and in some cases by their own party. The oversight of both legislatures, however, has seemed to pale into insignificance when ultimately compared to the power of the executive, whether through failure to gain impeachment proceedings or the attempt to prorogue the UK Parliament in September 2019.
- Both the US and UK executives have relied increasingly on those around them – aides in the USA and special advisers in the UK – rather than elected officials. However, elected officials in the UK seem to have remained more loyal to the executive than those in the USA in recent years.

Summary

The Mueller investigation is important because:

- The investigation into collusion between the Trump campaign and Russia, and obstruction of justice, despite lasting for over 2 years, ultimately failed to create a rallying point for either party.
- The complexity of the case has the potential to create apathy among many voters. The report, testimony and indictments seem to have created little political movement.

- It suggests that when the US political system is presented with unusual circumstances, such as the presidency of Donald Trump, there is enough flexibility to ensure that oversight is carried out, even by the executive branch itself.
- While the Constitution is often characterised as out-of-date and rigid, Congress and the executive branch have demonstrated an ability to use both enumerated and implied powers (see Chapter 6) in order to try to keep political power in balance.
- The Mueller investigation may not have provided ground-breaking headlines, but that in itself perhaps suggests the ability of US government to ensure that some level of normalcy is maintained even in the most unusual times.

Further reading and research

- Clarify your understanding by reading 'Special counsel: What is it and what did Robert Mueller investigate?' (www.bbc.co.uk).
- Read 'These are the 10 episodes Mueller investigated for obstruction of justice', which shows extracts from the Mueller report (www.vox.com). Does there appear to be enough evidence to indict President Trump for obstruction of justice once he leaves office?
- Create a diagram showing those who have been fired from or left the Trump administration since January 2017, and why.
- Aiming for an A? Read 'Mueller hearing: Have we learned anything new?' (www.bbc.co.uk) and evaluate whether the Mueller report had any impact on President Trump's chances of re-election in 2020.

Chapter 3

The Trump administration

Exam success

Article II of the US Constitution vests all executive power in 'a President'. It is crucial that students understand that, despite this, the 'presidency' is a huge branch of government. While many of the holders of the top jobs are appointed by the president, such as heads of departments, most of the federal bureaucracy (equivalent to the civil service in the UK) are non-political appointments. These people will have been in post long before the current president, and are likely to be in post long after him. This means that bodies within the presidency, such as departments, can have their own momentum and policy direction which does not always align with that of the president. Evidence of this can be seen within the Trump administration from the sheer volume of staff turnover in this branch.

The best students will understand that there are some unique elements to the Trump administration, but also some features common to most presidencies. His top advisers, while often changing, have demonstrated similar power to their predecessors in their roles.

AQA	3.2.1.3	The executive branch of government: relationships between the presidency and other institutions, and why this varies
Edexcel	3.2	Informal sources of presidential power and their use
	3.3.2	Limitations on presidential powers and why this varies
	3.4	Interpretations and debates of the US presidency: the imperial presidency

Context

The term 'the Trump administration' refers to the executive branch of the federal government under President Donald Trump. This includes the cabinet and the Executive Office of the President, as well as the executive departments, agencies and bureaus.

Every president since George Washington has appointed something that has been referred to as a 'cabinet', although the term does not appear in the Constitution. By the cabinet we mean the advisory group selected by the president to aid him in making decisions and coordinating the work of the federal bureaucracy. Because in this chapter we are making comparisons between the cabinets of different presidents, the term here will mean the heads of the executive departments — of which there are currently 15. Other people are given cabinet rank by the president but this varies from one administration to another.

The Executive Office of the President (EXOP) is the umbrella term for the top staff agencies in the White House that assist the president in carrying out the major responsibilities of his office. The main offices within EXOP are: the White House Office (headed by the chief of staff), the Office of Management and Budget (OMB) and the National Security Council (NSC).

White House–cabinet relations

The Trump administration is not the first to experience fractious relations between those who work in the White House and members of the president's cabinet — the two leading parts of the administration. The trouble is that they have different perspectives. The White House staff have only one client — the president — and that is especially true when that president is someone who places a high priority on loyalty, as Donald Trump does. The cabinet, on the other hand, has multiple clients — Congress that votes its budgets; the bureaucracy that does its day-to-day work; interest groups related to the work of its specific department; and then there's the president who hired the cabinet members and may fire them. As a result, presidents — and those who work in the White House — soon come to regard the cabinet as disloyal and semi-detached. In the words of one staff member in President Nixon's White House, cabinet members go off and 'marry the natives'.

The White House staff also have the huge advantage of proximity. They work at the White House. Indeed, the most important among them will work in the West Wing — the small, two-storey building which also houses the Oval Office. They will see the president on a regular basis. They get to know what the president wants right now, rather than what someone said he wanted a week or two ago. Unlike UK cabinet ministers, who see the prime minister almost every day parliament is in session — in the House of Commons — US cabinet officers have no regular or obvious way of seeing the president. Yes, there are cabinet meetings, but not usually as regularly or as frequently as in the British system. Furthermore, cabinet officers don't work in the White House. Many of them — like the secretary of defense — work a good way away from the White House. The only way they get to see the president is if he sends for them or they are given permission by the president's chief of staff to come to the Oval Office to see him. That may be reasonably frequently for someone like the secretary of state (foreign secretary) or the secretary of defense, but what if you are the secretary of the interior

(federal parks, natural resources, etc.)? So it is not surprising when things turn sour between the president and his staff and those who work outside the White House in downtown Washington.

But in the Trump administration, there is plentiful evidence already that relations between the White House and many in the President's cabinet are about as bad as they get. In his recent book *Fear: Trump in the White House* (Simon & Schuster, 2018) the veteran political reporter Bob Woodward tells of a meeting at the White House between the then Secretary of State Rex Tillerson and national security adviser H. R. McMaster:

> Tillerson: You guys in the White House don't have your act together. The President can't make a decision. He makes a decision and then changes his mind a couple of days later.

> McMaster: You don't work with the White House. You never consult me or anybody on the National Security Council staff. You are off doing your own thing.

> Tillerson: That's not true. I'm available any time. I talk to you all the time. We had a conference call yesterday. But I've got to be secretary of state. Sometimes I'm travelling. Sometimes I'm in a different time zone. I can't always take your calls.

And these two were meant to be on the same team, supporting the same policies, the same president!

Cabinet ins and outs

In terms of personnel, President Trump's cabinet is the most unstable in modern times — maybe ever. Even disregarding the acting cabinet officers whom Trump is fond of using, there were ten changes in Trump's cabinet between January 2017 and October 2019 — a period of 33 months (see Table 3.1). That is more than in a similar period for any elected president going back as far as John F. Kennedy (1961–63). The previous high during that period was the seven changes in the first 3 years of Jimmy Carter's administration, 40 years ago. Include Trump's use of acting secretaries, plus one nomination which was withdrawn, and there were 17 personnel changes among the 15 heads of the executive departments during the first 33 months of the Trump presidency. In anyone's book, that is an extraordinary level of instability. During the same period in the Obama administration (2009–11), there were just two cabinet personnel changes — and one of those was the departure of Secretary of Defense Robert Gates, who was a holdover appointment from the George W. Bush administration. During the same period in the George W. Bush administration (2001–03), there was just one change (see Figure 3.1).

Table 3.1 Personnel changes in President Trump's cabinet, 2017–19

Post	Out	In	Senate vote
Secretary of State	Rex Tillerson	Mike Pompeo	57–42
Secretary of Defense	James Mattis	Patrick Shanahan	*Acting
	Patrick Shanahan	Mark Esper	*Acting
	Mark Esper	Richard Spencer	*Acting
	Richard Spencer	Mark Esper	90–8
Attorney General	Jeff Sessions	Matthew Whitaker	*Acting
	Matthew Whitaker	William Barr	54–45
Secretary of the Interior	Ryan Zinke	David Bernhardt	56–41
Secretary of Labor	Alex Acosta	Eugene Scalia	53–44
Secretary of Health	Tom Price	Alex Azar	53–43
Secretary of Veterans' Affairs	David Shulkin	Ronny Jackson	Withdrawn
	Ronny Jackson	Robert Wilkie	86–9
Secretary of Homeland Security	John Kelly	Elaine Duke	*Acting
	Elaine Duke	Kirstjen Nielsen	62–37
	Kirstjen Nielsen	Kevin McAleenan	*Acting
	Kevin McAleenan	Chad Wolf	*Acting
Secretary of Energy	Rick Perry	†	

* not subject to Senate confirmation
† nomination awaited

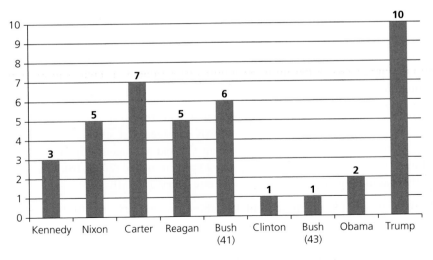

Figure 3.1 Cabinet officer changes during first 3 years of presidency

The reasons why people left Trump's cabinet fell into two groups: those with whom Trump fell out personally; and those who became embroiled in scandal. Those in the first group included Rex Tillerson, James Mattis, Jeff Sessions and Kirstjen

Nielsen. The way most of these fell out with the President was by failing to display the absolute loyalty that Trump demands of his appointees. Trump had told one incoming member of his administration: 'It's great that you went to Harvard and Oxford; you're smart and everybody vouches for you. But what really matters to me is that you're going to be loyal to me.' When that loyalty was — at least from the President's viewpoint — not forthcoming, it wasn't long before they were fired, sometimes in a tweet, as happened to Rex Tillerson.

Those who became too controversial and, as a consequence, either were fired or resigned included:

- Ryan Zinke: numerous financial and ethical issues
- Tom Price: spending over $1 million of departmental money on private and military jet flights
- David Shulkin: spending time sightseeing and shopping with his wife on a taxpayer-funded trip to Europe

For a president who in his election campaign repeatedly claimed that he would 'drain the swamp' of sleaze and unethical behaviour in Washington, this was quite a list.

The trouble with all this coming and going in the Trump cabinet is the lack of policy and administrative continuity. Even before Trump's third year was up, the Homeland Security department was on its fifth secretary, Defense on its fourth and Justice on its third.

Cabinet meetings

Cabinet meetings had received a mixed press in previous administrations. The main reason for this is that there is no doctrine of collective responsibility in the American president's cabinet. Cabinet officers are policy specialists and have no interest or expertise in anything outside their own departmental policy area. So there's no point having the secretary of defense, for example, listen to a discussion of education policy.

As a result, cabinet meetings tend to be somewhat rare and sporadic events in most administrations. President George W. Bush averaged just six cabinet meetings a year during his 8 years in office. President Obama averaged only between three and four. Indeed, in the whole of his last 2 years in office (2015–16), Obama held just five cabinet meetings — that is about one every 5 months!

By contrast, President Trump held 18 cabinet meetings in his first 2 years (see Table 3.2). Except for the time in the first half of 2017 when the President was still assembling his cabinet, full cabinet meetings were held on an almost monthly basis from June 2017 to February 2019 — 19 meetings in 21 months. We haven't seen that frequency of cabinet meetings since the early 1980s under President Ronald Reagan.

Table 3.2 Trump cabinet meetings, 2017–19

2017	2018	2019
1 13 March	**10** 10 January	**19** 2 January
2 12 June	**11** 8 March	**20** 12 February
3 31 July	**12** 9 April	**21** 16 July
4 9 September	**13** 9 May	**22** 21 October
5 16 October	**14** 21 June	**23** 19 November
6 1 November	**15** 18 July	
7 20 November	**16** 16 August	
8 6 December	**17** 18 October	
9 20 December	**18** 1 November	

But activity isn't the same as achievement. In other words, just because there are a lot of cabinet meetings under President Trump doesn't of itself mean that these meetings are useful or are achieving anything. Let's take one of the cabinet meetings from 2019 as an example — the one that met on 16 July. We know all about it because members of the press — who are normally allowed to remain only for the first few minutes of a cabinet meeting — were on this occasion allowed to remain throughout. That in itself tells you something about the meeting. Trump clearly sees cabinet meetings primarily not as a deliberative, problem-solving or advice-giving events, but as public relations exercises. He might think the country will be reassured when they see the President meeting with his top administration officials.

From reading the transcript of this cabinet meeting, you find out five other things about Trump cabinet meetings:

1 They are used by the President to trumpet what he sees as his successes, though usually in a very generalised manner. So, for example, at this meeting we read that according to the President:
   - 'Our unemployment numbers are historic' (historically low, that is!)
   - 'We've got an extraordinary country. We've got numbers that have never been done before.'
   - 'Our country is doing things that nobody thought would even be possible. We're doing incredibly well.'

2 They are used by cabinet officers to congratulate the President. So, for example, when Secretary of Housing and Urban Development (HUD) Ben Carson was asked to speak, his opening words were:
   - 'And just before I talk a little bit about what's going on at HUD, I just want to thank you, Mr President, for your incredible courage, and stamina, and resilience with unfair criticism, all of the time.'

3 They are used by the President to congratulate his cabinet members. So, for example:

- the President said that Secretary of Agriculture Sonny Perdue has 'done a fantastic job'
- after HUD Secretary Ben Carson had spoken, the President commented: 'Fantastic job. Beautiful words. We appreciate it. Thank you Ben. Really good job.'

4 Most cabinet officers don't participate. On this occasion, other than Carson only three heads of departments spoke: Secretary of State Mike Pompeo, Secretary of Health and Human Services Alex Azar and Secretary of Labor Alex Acosta (because it was his last meeting).

5 There does not appear to be an agenda. At one point, the President announced that 'we're going round the table', presumably to give each member a chance to summarise what was going on in their department, but this never actually happened. After Labor Secretary Acosta had said his farewells, the President threw it open to the press to ask (him) questions, before closing the meeting. The meeting lasted exactly 77 minutes.

Cabinet meetings in the United States have never been hugely important. There are ways a president can make them useful: to chivvy members to get legislation through Congress; to sort out inter-departmental disputes; to brief them on big ticket policies. But so long as Trump sees cabinet meetings as merely a PR exercise — in much the same way as President Nixon did — they will almost certainly remain a largely policy-free zone.

White House staff

Just as in the cabinet, the Trump White House has seen a huge turnover in membership (see Table 3.3), and Trump's passion for loyalty is clearly a factor. As Anthony Scaramucci — who briefly held the post of White House Director of Communications — stated recently of those who worked in the Trump White House:

> You're there more as an annoyance to him because he has to fill some of these jobs, but you're not there to do anything other than backlighting. He wants a catatonic loyalty, and he wants you to be behind the backlights. There's only one spotlight on the stage, and it's shining on Trump, and you're just a prop in the back with dim lights.

Indeed, turnover in the Trump administration is inevitable, given the degree of loyalty the President requires of anyone to survive. But second, they must not get a good press. Someone who has worked at the Trump White House put it this way:

> There are those aides whose demise is all but a foregone conclusion, the result of the President's coming to suspect that an adviser thinks he or she is smarter than he is or is trying to undermine him in some way.

That was why Trump's third national security adviser John Bolton was fired or resigned (depending on whether you believe Trump's or Bolton's version of events) in September 2019. One of Bolton's fatal mistakes was that he sometimes tried to outsmart the President and get his own hawkish worldview enacted over the President's agenda. Once Trump was tipped off by his loyal acolytes as to what Bolton was up to — briefing the press and lobbying Congress behind the President's back — his days were numbered.

Table 3.3 Selected resignations and firings from the Trump administration, 2017–19

Date	Name	Resigned/fired as
2017		
13 February	Michael Flynn	National Security Adviser
21 July	Sean Spicer	White House Press Secretary
31 July	Reince Priebus	White House Chief of Staff
31 July	Anthony Scaramucci	White House Director of Communications
18 August	Steve Bannon	Chief Strategist
2018		
7 February	Rob Porter	White House Staff Secretary
13 March	Gary Cohn	Director, National Economic Council
29 March	Hope Hicks	White House Director of Communications
9 April	H. R. McMaster	National Security Adviser
10 April	Tom Bossert	Homeland Security Adviser
20 July	Marc Short	Director, Office of Legislative Affairs
17 October	Don McGahn	White House Counsel
2019		
2 January	John Kelly	White House Chief of Staff
8 March	Bill Shine	White House Director of Communications
30 June	Sarah Sanders	White House Press Secretary
15 July	Kevin Hassett	Chairman, Council of Economic Advisers
10 September	John Bolton	National Security Adviser

Of course, in one way, President Trump was right to dismiss any member of his staff who was trying to subvert his agenda by promoting their own priorities. Those who work in the White House are supposed to have 'a passion for anonymity'. But then that raises another question: why were these people appointed in the first place? Did the President really think that John Bolton, for example, would suddenly be happy to operate in the White House as a behind-the-scenes facilitator?

All of this raises serious questions for President Trump as he enters a critical fourth year in office. Leon Panetta, who has served both as Secretary of Defense and White House Chief of Staff in previous Democratic administrations, thinks that Trump's managerial style brings dangers. 'The presidency is an isolated position to begin with, and it is incredibly important to have people around you who will tell you when they think you're wrong,' Panetta told the *Washington Post* in a recent interview. 'Presidents need to appreciate that information and not then take it out on the individual. This president has a real blind spot in that he does not want anybody around him who is critical.' Such a strategy may work for a short time, and while things are going well, but eventually it can breed a 'them and us' atmosphere in the White House and sour relationships within the administration, with the Congress and eventually with the voters. That way holds dangers for the President in 2020.

Comparison

In both the USA and the UK, the role of those surrounding the executive has faced increasing scrutiny in recent political circumstances.

- Both the US and UK cabinets have experienced a very high level of staff turnover, despite extensive differences in how and why cabinet members are appointed. Whilst US cabinet members are expected to be experts in their field, appointments to the UK cabinet are more political. Yet, both models have faced significant challenges in retaining staff.
- Both the US and UK executives have seen growing challenges to their authority from their cabinet. In the UK, a series of hung parliaments, coalitions and small majorities have meant that the cabinet is more fractured than ever and cabinet collective responsibility seems to be less and less significant. Similarly, both presidents Trump and Obama have faced severe and vocal criticism from their own cabinet appointees over a range of issues. Whilst there is no cabinet collective responsibility in the USA, such criticism is unusual.
- Both the US and UK executives have placed increasing powers in those around them who do not hold a political office for which they are accountable. Nick Timothy and Fiona Hill were noted for their role in the calling of the 2017 election in the UK, whilst appointments such as Stephen Miller in EXOP court controversy by the way they represent the Trump administration in the media.

Summary

In this chapter we have covered the following issues:

- The relationships between those who work in the Trump White House and those who run the executive departments of the federal government.
- The comings and goings — including the unusually high rate of turnover — among these heads of the executive departments, collectively known as the president's cabinet.
- The frequency of Trump cabinet meetings and how they are used by the President.
- Turnover among the senior Trump White House team as well as the pros and cons of Trump's managerial style.

Further reading and research

You can find out about the comings and goings in both the Trump cabinet and the White House by regularly visiting the websites of major news media in the USA such as:

- **www.washingtonpost.com**
- **www.nytimes.com**

There is also the White House website at **www.whitehouse.gov.**

To research the latest Trump cabinet meetings, go to the search button at the top right-hand corner of the White House website's home page and type in 'cabinet meetings'. This will display a transcript of the President's press statements at the start of recent cabinet meetings.

You can also type 'Trump cabinet meetings' into the Google search engine and then press 'Videos'. This will bring up video coverage of all the latest Trump cabinet meetings.

Chapter 4

Immigration

Exam success

Immigration does not exist as a standalone topic in the specifications for A-level Politics, but it will enhance essay answers on the topic of civil rights and how effectively they have been protected. It is crucial, therefore, that students do not confuse civil rights and human rights. Illegal immigrants trying to cross into the USA are not entitled to protection under the US Constitution as they are not citizens and therefore civil rights do not necessarily apply to them. In these cases, the topic of immigration can be used to consider the powers of the three major branches of government — Congress, the president and the Supreme Court — and the power of states in choosing how they react to illegal immigrants. President Trump's actions regarding the USA–Mexico 'Wall' is a good case study. His separation of families and willingness to declare a national emergency to obtain the funding he wanted can both be seen as representative of a powerful, if somewhat irreverent, president.

For long-term immigrants who live in the USA, and often have done for decades, it is far easier to discuss whether their rights are adequately protected. While they may not hold legal status, many have jobs, pay taxes or have children who were born in the USA. The extent to which their rights are protected is often viewed through the willingness or otherwise of the government to pass laws to protect them, and the willingness of the Supreme Court to rule in favour of their rights. President Obama's DAPA and DACA executive orders were aimed at these groups, and the rescinding of them by President Trump shows less willingness to distinguish between these types of immigrants.

AQA	3.2.1.8	Civil rights
	3.2.1.4	The judicial branch: Supreme Court as a protector of citizens' rights
Edexcel	4.4.5	Race and rights in contemporary US politics
	4.4	The protection of civil liberties and rights in the US today

Context

Immigration has long been an issue on which the president, Congress and Supreme Court, as well as the individual states, have all passed opinions. Immigration from Mexico has been declining since the middle of the presidency of George W. Bush. President Obama struggled to get meaningful immigration reform through Congress. While a bipartisan group of eight Senators, the 'Gang of 8', created a reform bill, it was rejected by the House of

Representatives. Obama cracked down on illegal immigration and deported more than 2.5 million people — more than any other president in history — to demonstrate to Congress that he could be trusted on the issue. He succeeded only in earning himself the title of 'Deporter-in-Chief' from the Latino rights group the Council of La Raza (now UnidosUS), and so resorted instead to using executive orders.

President Trump's administration has made immigration a key policy area — the cause of a government shutdown, a declaration of national emergency and a damning cover of *TIME* magazine. The President has frequently circumvented, vetoed and challenged Congress on the issue, while relying on the support of the newly conservative-leaning Supreme Court. However, his policies have not gone unchallenged. Some cities have declared themselves sanctuary cities and launched legal bids against his policies, Congress passed a joint resolution against the declaration of a national emergency and the Supreme Court prevented Trump adding a question about citizenship to the census.

Immigration at the Mexican border

Even before winning the office of the president, Trump was campaigning for a wall along the USA–Mexico border to curb immigration. Just 5 days into his presidency, he signed an executive order calling for the construction of this wall. In the months that followed he rescinded the Obama-era Deferred Action for Parents of Americans (DAPA) executive order, although the Supreme Court ultimately prevented him from ending Deferred Action for Childhood Arrivals (DACA) too. Despite the bluster and rhetoric, progress on the wall seemed slow, although the Republicans held both houses of Congress from 2017 to 2019. With Democrats taking the House in 2019, the power of the President has been brought further into question over the issue of immigration.

Separation of families

On 6 April 2018, then Attorney General Jeff Sessions issued a memorandum stating that there would be a 'zero tolerance' approach to illegal immigration to the USA. A follow-up statement on 7 May 2018 specifically targeted those crossing the USA–Mexico border with children (see Box 4.1). This statement set out that illegal entry to the USA would be met with the full force of the law and those smuggling children would be separated from them. It began a media crisis for President Trump that would see the policy rescinded in just over 2 months.

Box 4.1	**Memorandum from Attorney Jeff Sessions, 7 May 2019**

I have put in place a 'zero tolerance' policy for illegal entry on our Southwest border. If you cross this border unlawfully, then we will prosecute you. It's that simple. If you smuggle illegal aliens across our border, then we will prosecute you. **If you are smuggling a child, then we will prosecute you and that child will be separated from you as required by law**... So if you're going to come to this country, come here legally. Don't come here illegally.

What followed in the media was a series of images from the USA–Mexico border of crying children being separated from their families and stories of them being caged and kept in inhumane conditions. The stark image of a young girl crying was used on the front cover of *TIME* magazine alongside President Trump and the title 'Welcome to America.' While President Trump has grown accustomed to weathering storms about his public image, the negativity of reporting on this issue led to an executive order on 20 June 2018 purportedly ending the separation of families.

In both initiating and ending the policy, however, Trump demonstrated the power of the presidency as an institution. The use of memoranda and executive orders (see Box 4.2) circumvented Congress and the checks and balances between the branches of government, and enabled the Trump administration to put in place a policy that the executive alone wished to follow. The crucial effect of reporting in the media, some of which reported congressional objections to the policy, could arguably be said to demonstrate the weakness of Congress in providing effective oversight of the presidency.

Box 4.2 Executive orders

Executive orders are *not* new laws, and cannot be. Only Congress, as the legislative branch, has the power and right to make legislation under the US Constitution. Rather, executive orders are directions from the president to the relevant department about how he would like a specific law to be implemented. While many presidents may appear to use executive orders to create quasi-law and sidestep Congress, it is crucial to understand that such orders merely interpret existing law.

Furthermore, while nearly 1,500 children had been reunited with their families by July 2018, nearly a further 1,000 remained separated. Indeed, whether the policy was truly ended at this point remains an issue of contention with numerous reports of its continuation emerging through 2019.

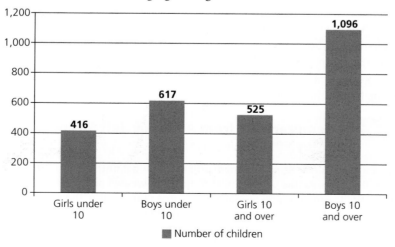

Figure 4.1 Age and gender of 2,654 children separated from their parents

The executive order that President Trump signed in June was entitled, 'Affording Congress an Opportunity To Address Family Separation'. Such a title is both powerful and bitterly ironic. On the one hand, it highlighted a substantial number of the limitations that a president can face. The order showed deference by the presidency to Congress as the only body which can pass legislation. It highlighted that the presidency was actually enforcing a congressional law: the Immigration and Nationality Act of 1965. It also demonstrated the fragility of executive orders, which can so easily be reversed from one president to the next or indeed more frequently.

The judicial challenge

Equally, the presidency was further limited when a federal judge in a US district court ordered that families that had been separated must be reunited. Judge Dana Sabraw ruled that children under 5 years old must be reunited within 14 days, and those older than this must be reunited within 30 days. This is a clear example of the US courts being willing to step in and defend the rights of immigrants, even illegal immigrants, against the presidency. Nonetheless, the court order was not enough to ensure that all children have been reunited as some lack the paper trail needed to be able to reunite them with their family — something that the federal judge lambasted Trump's administration for (see Box 4.3). The court case was brought by the American Civil Liberties Union (ACLU) on behalf of those who had been separated, demonstrating the ability of both the US courts and interest groups to protect the rights of immigrants.

> ### Box 4.3 US District Court Judge Dana Sabraw's comments requiring the reuniting of children with their families
>
> The government readily keeps track of personal property of detainees in criminal and immigration proceedings. Money, important documents, and automobiles, to name a few, are routinely catalogued, stored, tracked and produced upon a detainee's release, at all levels — state and federal, citizen and alien. Yet, the government has no system in place to keep track of, provide effective communication with, and promptly produce alien children. **The unfortunate reality is that under the present system migrant children are not accounted for with the same efficiency and accuracy as property**. Certainly, that cannot satisfy the requirements of due process.

Challenges from the states

Further to this, and another challenge by the ACLU, 17 states also launched a legal challenge to the separation of families. The fact that this challenge was launched over a week after the executive order that supposedly ended the practice suggests that they had little faith in the executive order. Many of these states were liberal leaning and contained sanctuary cities (cities that refused to enforce federal immigration policies at state level, effectively offering sanctuary to immigrants).

Importantly, this challenge was launched using the US Constitution, despite defending illegal immigrants. The 17 states claimed that Trump's policy violated the Fifth Amendment to the Constitution, guaranteeing due process. Such a challenge is a substantial demonstration of the limitations of the presidency in a federal system where sovereignty is shared between federal and state government. Not only can the presidency be challenged by states, but it is also reliant on states to enforce its policies. The detention centres in which the separated children were held were spread across the USA and therefore depended at least in part on the compliance of the states.

The congressional challenge

Congress also took to challenging the President on this issue. In a less effective method than a legal challenge, a number of Democratic senators wrote letters to Trump demanding to know the number of children being held in custody. These letters, however, barely made headlines and legally required no action from President Trump. More importantly, Congress made use of its constitutional 'power of the purse'. It added amendments to the bill that funded the Department of Health and Human Services (HHS), requiring updates on the number of children being held as part of the financial deal. While Congress had little ability to force an end to the executive order, it was nonetheless able to utilise some of its powers to try to bring the situation under control and demand information on its resolution.

The presidential reaction

On the other hand however, whilst the crisis was effectively limited if not brought to an end by pressure from a range of political actors, the administration's ability to launch it with little oversight demonstrates the power that the presidency has, especially over issues that could be deemed to be 'foreign policy'. The executive order ending the separation of families was explicit in stating that 'Congress's failure to act and court orders have put the Administration in the position of separating alien families to effectively enforce the law'. Even in ending the policy, therefore, the Trump administration placed the blame at the door of Congress.

The executive order, importantly, did not end the practice of detention. In the headlines generated by Trump signing this order, the focus was very clearly on ending the policy of separation of families. While the executive order did maintain that families would no longer be separated, however, they would still be detained, merely together. Nor did the order address the conditions in which detainees were held. Given this eventuality, the administration still effectively achieved its goal of being able to detain those crossing the border.

Furthermore, former Homeland Security Secretary Kirstjen Nielsen suggested that, even after the policy was officially ended by the executive order, Trump was pushing the department to re-implement the separations. This is an important reminder that, while the president alone is given executive power in the Constitution, the presidential branch is an enormous machine. Nielsen was speaking after her resignation from the role of a cabinet secretary and was purportedly opposed to the harsh policies. However, her resignation reflects the administration's attempts to ensure that those in such posts support a harsher approach to immigration. This reflects the importance of the Executive Office of the President (EXOP) to the president, often over and above the cabinet or departments, with top White House adviser Stephen Miller being in part responsible for the hard-line approach to immigration.

The entire episode served as a precursor to the longest government shutdown in US history from December 2018 to January 2019, and the subsequent declaration of a national emergency, both over the issue of immigration along the USA–Mexico border. Therefore, while one policy of the presidency may have been limited, the President was simply able to deploy other powers that he has to achieve his policy goals. This seems to be a common outcome under the presidency of Donald Trump – far from being chastened in defeat, he is able to use the power of the presidency to find other routes to his policy goals. Tentatively, his approach could be likened to losing the battle in order to win the war!

The shutdown and the national emergency

Power of the purse

In the months that followed the separation of families' crisis, the issue of immigration remained high on the Trump administration's agenda. One way the administration attempted to pursue this agenda was through the budget for the 2019 fiscal year. Congress's 'power of the purse' means it has the final say on passing a budget for the US government. However, this power has been notoriously difficult to exercise in recent years. In fact, between 2002 and 2016 only seven budgets were adopted. The gap that this creates in the country's accounts is often bridged through the use of 'continuing resolutions'. This is effectively an agreement to continue funding for the government as it is until a budget agreement can be reached.

With a failure to agree a budget for 2019, or to agree on a continuing resolution, the US government went into shutdown on 22 December 2018, and remained shut down for 35 days, the longest in US history. The key cause of the tension between the presidency and Congress in agreeing a budget was the allocation of $5 billion for a wall along the USA–Mexico border demanded by President Trump.

The shutdown eventually ended on 25 January 2019 when President Trump agreed to a temporary financial agreement that did not include the money for his wall. This demonstrated the power that Congress still holds with regard to the 'power of the purse'. However, the immense standoff equally demonstrates the power of the President to frustrate the efforts of Congress, resulting in gridlock in US government. It is therefore difficult to argue that either side is effectively powerful when their efforts to block each other lead to an impasse where no one can exercise any power at all. It also demonstrates the difficulty of achieving meaningful policy in an age of hyper-partisanship, where a divided government means that such standoffs are increasingly likely.

Challenging the power of the purse

A bipartisan funding bill was eventually passed by Congress and the President but did not include funding for the proposed wall. Instead it included $1.375 billion for a steel fence along the border. On the same day that President Trump signed this bill, he also declared a 'National Emergency Concerning the Southern Border of the United States'. This allowed him to redirect money already pledged to the US government to the border wall that he wanted and meant a total of around $8 billion became available for the project.

Democrats in Congress reacted angrily to this declaration, saying that Trump's actions 'clearly violate the Congress's exclusive power of the purse, which our founders enshrined in the Constitution'. They suggested that this controversy would be dealt with in the courts and Trump himself said he expected to be sued. However, with Trump having appointed two conservative-leaning justices to the Supreme Court by this time, when the case did reach the Supreme Court, Trump's declaration was upheld, highlighting the importance of the power that the President has in appointing Supreme Court justices who share a similar ideology to his own.

Congress also reacted by passing a joint resolution to end the national emergency, but Trump used his first veto in order to prevent the resolution from passing. Considering fiscal matters are explicitly placed within the power of Congress in the Constitution, that neither Congress nor the Supreme Court was able to prevent President Trump from enacting a national emergency in order to achieve his policy goals suggests a substantial imbalance of power in the system of checks and balances, and again suggests a powerful presidency in the area of foreign policy. It especially demonstrates the importance of an imperial power – one that lacks effective checks and balances – such as the veto for the president. Neither chamber had the votes to be able to overturn the veto, so the veto remained in place.

The Supreme Court

The newly conservative-leaning Supreme Court also played a key role in the immigration debate that exploded in 2018–19. Several key cases, decided both for and against President Trump, served further to change the landscape of the immigration debate.

Department of Commerce v *New York*, 2019

The Trump administration wanted to add a question to the 2020 census asking whether the respondents were US citizens. When evidence came to light that the motive behind this was to gain more support for Republicans, the Supreme Court decided 5–4 that it was not allowed. It referred the case back to the lower courts, however, commenting that if better evidence was provided that the question was necessary, the issue could be reconsidered. While this could be considered a victory for immigrants' rights, Trump said that the data would instead be gathered through the use of executive orders, suggesting once again a willingness to use a range of presidential powers to achieve his policy goals.

Nielsen v *Preap*, 2019

The Supreme Court decided 5–4 that the federal government had the right to detain non-citizens at any time if they had previously committed a crime, even if that crime was years in the past. This could be considered a failure to protect immigrants' rights, and again demonstrates the considerable importance of ideology in the Supreme Court, with the conservatives (Alito, Thomas, Roberts, Gorsuch and Kavanaugh) forming the majority. It also underlines the importance of the two conservative appointments made to the Supreme Court by President Trump.

Agreeing to hear DACA

Whilst President Trump was able to end Obama's DAPA programme, he faced a block from the judiciary when he tried to end DACA. The Supreme Court finally agreed to hear the 2-year-long dispute in June 2019 – *Department of Homeland Security* v *Regents of the University of California et al*. With the case to be heard during 2019–20, it remains to be seen whether the Court will side with the President or not, and whether it will divide along ideological lines or not.

Comparison

In both the USA and the UK, immigration has been a key policy area in 2018–19, as a result of the USA–Mexico border and the impact of Brexit.

- Both the USA and the UK have seen strong executives pushing conservative policies on immigration and conflicting with their legislatures. While Trump vetoed Congress's effort to rebuke him, Prime Minister Johnson attempted to prorogue Parliament in order to achieve the harder Brexit that he wanted.
- Both the USA and the UK have seen pressure group action in the wider context of these issues. The actual method, however, is very different. While the ACLU in the USA has made broad use of the US Supreme Court, the UK has seen vast protests on the streets and e-petitions to prevent the prorogation, which will directly affect the rights that EU immigrants in the UK end up with in a Brexit deal.
- Both the USA and the UK have seen challenges launched against the national government – by the states in the USA and the devolved powers in the UK. These have been launched by geographical areas whose ideologies directly contrast with that of the central government, and both have used the judicial system to do this.

Summary

The central focus of the immigration debate is not simply about the protection of rights of immigrants, but over who protects their rights and how effectively.

- The immigration debate does demonstrate that in the area of foreign policy, President Trump has been able work through a range of different channels to achieve his goals, and at the very least is effective at creating stalemate to avoid losing too much ground in this debate.
- The protection of immigrants' rights in the US is especially political given the politicised nature of the courts, and especially as the Supreme Court sways between liberal- or conservative-leaning, the protection of rights can vary immensely.
- Nonetheless, the challenges to a president, even in this dominant area, are significant. The rhetoric of President Trump must be carefully analysed, as Congress, the Supreme Court, states and pressure groups have all more or less successfully launched challenges to his immigration policy.

Further reading and research

- Read 'Trump issues first veto of his presidency' by Eliana Johnson and Katie Galioto, 15 March 2019 (**www.politico.com**).
- Create your own timeline of the development of immigration policy in the USA using the 'Timeline of federal policy on immigration 2017–2020' on **www.ballotpedia.org**.
- Create a case study of the *Department of Homeland Security* v *Regents of the University of California* as the case emerges.
- Aiming for an A? Read the 'executive summary' of 'US immigration policy under Trump: Deep changes and lasting impacts' on **www.migrationpolicy.org**. Does this suggest that the Trump presidency is more imperial or imperilled by the action of other branches?

Chapter 5

Trump and the imperial presidency

Context

The term was coined by the Pulitzer prize-winning historian Arthur Schlesinger when he published a book entitled *The Imperial Presidency* in 1974. That was the year in which President Nixon was forced to resign over what came to be known as the Watergate affair. Schlesinger's book focused on the six presidents

who held office from 1933 to 1974 — Franklin Roosevelt, Harry Truman, Dwight Eisenhower, John Kennedy, Lyndon Johnson and Richard Nixon. Schlesinger claimed that 'the imperial presidency was born in the 1940s and 1950s to save the world from perdition' — by which he principally meant the Axis powers of Germany, Italy and Japan — but that this gave rise to a form of imperial presidency in domestic policy in the 1960s and 1970s. Since then, the term has been much debated in terms of how well it describes each subsequent president.

According to Schlesinger, the imperial presidency had four main characteristics:

- power
- secrecy
- dislike of the press
- illegality

Schlesinger suggested that these characteristics of the imperial presidency were evident in President Johnson's conduct of the Vietnam War and in President Nixon's handling of Watergate — both its execution and the subsequent attempted cover-up. Given these characteristics, in this chapter we shall seek to determine to what extent the Trump presidency fits the description of the imperial presidency during its first 3 years.

Trump and presidential power

President Trump, of course, has the same powers as all his immediate predecessors. Indeed, most of his powers — to recommend legislation, to nominate executive and judicial branch officials, to veto legislation, to act as commander-in-chief — are the powers that George Washington had back in the eighteenth century. Presidential powers (note the plural) are a constant. But presidential power (note the singular) is a variable. Presidential powers are the president's constitutional tasks, functions and duties. Presidential power is seen as the ability of the president to get what he wants. Different people — even different presidents — have different views on how powerful the president *should* be. Donald Trump has a high view of presidential power.

Speaking at a conference in Washington DC in July 2019 — just after the publication of the Mueller Report (see Chapter 2) — President Trump both criticised the Mueller investigation and repeated his (false) claim that the report had found 'no collusion, no obstruction'. The President continued: 'I have Article II, where I have the right to do whatever I want as president.' Neither was this the first time that Trump had made this claim. Clearly this is a very expansive view of Article II and of presidential power. Indeed, it is an incorrect view of both. Yes, Article II grants the president 'all executive power' but that is not the same as total power — 'do whatever I want'. Article II is the part of the Constitution that also describes many of Congress's checks on the president and gives Congress significant oversight powers. 'It's certainly not a grant of unlimited power,' commented William C. Banks, a law professor at Syracuse University. 'He's not a monarch, he's the chief executive, and he's bound to uphold the rule of law.' Trump, of course, is not the first president to take an expansive view of presidential power. But Trump's declaration of a state of emergency and his diverting of federal funds to start the building of his much-talked-about border wall between the USA and Mexico was probably the clearest example of the overt expansion of presidential power during 2019.

Trump and secrecy

To control information is to have power. To know things that others do not know, and want to know, is to have power. While some level of secrecy is a requirement of good government, even in a democracy, if the chief executive uses secrecy as a significant political tool to avoid scrutiny — by the legislature, the judiciary or the media — then there will soon be a concern that the constitutional system of checks and balances is being thwarted.

> **Box 5.1** **Some areas where President Trump has adopted a policy of secrecy**
>
> - Payments of more than $1000,000 that the President made to reimburse his lawyer, Michael Cohen, some of which was paid to porn star Stormy Daniels.
> - Failure to release his tax returns and fighting every attempt in Congress and the courts to make him release them.
> - Refusal to reveal changes made regarding use of lethal force in counter-terrorism operations.
> - Refusal to reveal business dealings abroad.
> - Initially blocked 'whistleblower' disclosure regarding a phone call Trump had with Ukraine's President Zelensky.
> - Defying numerous congressional subpoenas and telling members of his administration likewise to defy subpoenas.

For President Trump, things became more difficult once the Democrats took control of the House of Representatives in January 2019 — the start of his third year in office. For the first 2 years, the President had been less concerned to keep things secret from Congress. After all, with Republicans controlling both houses, and the Republican Party both in Washington and in the country having become pretty much a Trump party, the President had little to fear in terms of scrutiny by congressional committees.

But when in 2019 the Democrat-controlled House fired off subpoenas in an attempt to force the President to reveal information regarding some contentious issues (see Box 5.1), Trump vowed to resist 'all' subpoenas by House Democrats, portraying the Democrats' activities as 'presidential harassment'. Rep. Elijah Cummings, chairman of the House Oversight Committee, stated: 'Congress must have access to information we need to do our job effectively and efficiently, and we urge the President to stop engaging in this unprecedented cover-up and start complying with the law.' Although, again, President Trump is by no means the

first president to prefer secrecy to disclosure, he has taken the withholding of information from Congress further than many of his predecessors.

Trump and dislike of the press

The penchant for secrecy is linked with another characteristic of the imperial presidency: namely dislike and distrust of the press. Trump has repeatedly referred to the 'fake news' media and denigrated the work both of specific media organisations — CNN and *The New York Times* come to mind — and of individual journalists whom he regards as hostile. Trump is also often heard — especially in his partisan rallies — referring to the media in general as 'the enemy of the people'. It is rather reminiscent of President Nixon's 'enemies list' — a list of those whom the President refused to have invited to the White House. At a private event in New York in September 2019, on the day when the story of his phone call with the Ukrainian president was making all the headlines, Trump remarked to an assembled crowd: 'You know, these animals in the press. They're animals, some of the worst human beings you'll ever meet. They're scum. Many of them are scum, and then you have some good reporters, but not many of them.'

Table 5.1 Press appearances in first 31 months of presidency:
Obama and Trump compared

	Obama	Trump
Solo White House press conferences	17	2
Joint press conferences with foreign leaders	44	38
Other photo opportunities with shouted Q&As	24	205

Something not seen in previous administrations has been the demise of White House press briefings. In most recent administrations, these were almost daily (weekday) events covered live on cable TV, conducted by the president's press secretary. At the very start of the Trump presidency, these briefings were held with a similar degree of frequency, presided over by the Press Secretary, Sean Spicer. Later, under Spicer's replacement Sarah Sanders, these briefings fell to around one or two a week. By the beginning of 2019, they were down to an average of just one a month, and following her departure in July, they disappeared altogether, giving the appearance of a closed and secretive White House. Stephanie Grisham, who replaced Sanders as White House Press Secretary, held no formal press briefings during her first 5 months in office. Trump has also held far fewer solo White House press conferences than President Obama (see Table 5.1).

Instead, the President allows the press to shout questions at him as he is going to and from engagements. These are often conducted in the White House grounds against the background noise of the engine of Marine One — the presidential helicopter. This was a ploy used by President Reagan. Andrew Feinberg, a White House reporter for Breakfast Media, comments:

> They're structured in such a way that they're almost irrelevant. They keep the
> engine [on Marine One] running, which apparently they don't have to do, and

it's set up in a way the President can just wander up and down the rope line, picking the reporters he recognises off TV and the questions and topics he likes, while ignoring any question that might call for a little effort to put out a coherent answer. It's also hard for the audio to pick up the [reporters'] questions. People at home often don't hear it. It's a way for the President and administration to cloak themselves in the mantle of transparency while providing little useful information.

The President's defenders would point out that because he — rather than his press secretary — is answering the questions, President Trump is much more open to the press than many of his predecessors.

Illegality

No modern-day administration was so rife with unlawful and illegal behaviour as that of President Nixon (1969–74). Seven senior members of the Nixon administration — including his former chief of staff and attorney general — were indicted, and President Nixon himself was named as an unindicted co-conspirator by a grand jury. Nixon resigned and was then pardoned by his successor Gerald Ford. This, to many, was the height of the imperial presidency.

At the time of writing, nothing remotely on this scale is being suggested about the administration of President Trump (which is why this section has not been entitled 'Trump and illegality'.) Some have thought the tactics he used to suppress unflattering stories about him and his public denigration of anyone who opposes him — be they judges, the Special Counsel, Democratic members of Congress, or sometimes even serving or former members of his own administration (such as Attorney General Jeff Sessions) — have gone too far. But that is not the same as illegality.

Certainly President Trump has a tendency not to tell the truth. Examples are well documented. Certainly President Trump has broken the boundaries of what were previously thought of as accepted presidential norms. Certainly his presidency centres very much on him as a person. There is certainly more than a hint of the French king Louis XIV's claim, *'L'état, c'est moi'* ('I am the state') in some of Trump's pronouncements.

Impeachment

In September 2019, the Speaker of the House, Nancy Pelosi, announced that the Democrats in the House had opened a formal impeachment inquiry into President Trump (see Box 5.3). Impeachment (see Box 5.2) is the most significant check held by Congress on the president — yet it is also the most fraught with difficulty, and it can easily boomerang on the ones who launch it. That is exactly what happened to Republicans in Congress when they launched an impeachment of President Bill Clinton in 1998. True, they impeached the President, but they

went on to pay a political price for it in that year's midterm elections. Indeed, Clinton's opinion poll ratings rose steadily from the moment of his impeachment because many thought that the Republicans had over-reacted to the President's admittedly foolish behaviour. Could the same thing happen this time around with the parties reversed?

Box 5.2 Impeachment — what it is and how it works

Definition

A formal accusation of a serving federal official — in this case, the president — by a simple majority vote of the House of Representatives.

How it works

1 **Formal inquiry** (usually conducted by the House Judiciary Committee)
↓
2 **Committee drafts article(s) of impeachment**
↓
3 **House of Representatives debates each article on the floor of the House**
↓
4 **House votes on each article**
↓
5 **If one or more articles are passed by a simple majority, the president is impeached**
↓
6 **If President Trump is impeached, he would be tried in the Senate**
- Chief Justice John Roberts would preside.
- All 100 senators act as the jury.
- 67 votes are needed to convict.
- If convicted, Trump would be removed from office and the Vice President would become President.

Some words of caution

The 'imperial presidency' refers to a version of US government in which the conventional checks and balances between the three branches of the federal government — especially those between the Congress and the president — have got out of balance. The executive branch has become dominant; the legislature has become subservient. In the current era of partisanship, it is difficult to envisage a repeat of what happened in August 1974 — Republican members of Congress going to the White House to tell a Republican president that he had to resign or face certain impeachment, conviction and removal from office. In Washington today, the lines are drawn strictly along party lines. On one side of that line, President Trump is seen as a villain; on the other side, as a victim. It is therefore doubtful whether the constitutional check of impeachment will achieve much of great value.

Box 5.3 | Impeachment of President Trump

Background

- Until 2018 only two presidents had been impeached by the House of Representatives: Andrew Johnson (1868) and Bill Clinton (1998). Both were found not guilty by the Senate. In 1974, Richard Nixon resigned before the House could impeach him.
- Thus, on 18 December 2019, Donald Trump became the third president to be impeached when the House of Representatives passed two articles of impeachment against him.

Trump impeachment timeline

- 10 July 2019: US Ambassador to the EU Gordon Sondland in a West Wing meeting with two top Ukrainian advisers tried to pressure Ukraine to dig up political dirt on Democratic presidential candidate Joe Biden and his son Hunter Biden. Sondland appeared to have the support of both President Trump and Acting White House Chief of Staff Mick Mulvaney.
- 18 July: President Trump places $391 million of military aid to Ukraine on hold, but gives no explanation for this to senior members of his administration.
- 25 July: President Trump has a phone call with the recently elected Ukrainian president, Volodymyr Zelensky. In this call Trump reminds Zelensky that 'the United States has been very good to Ukraine' before asking, 'I would like you to do us a favour.' The 'favour' is to investigate the business dealings in Ukraine of Hunter Biden, the son of Democratic presidential candidate Joe Biden. In the call, the President says that he will get Attorney General William Barr and Rudy Giuliani to liaise with Zelensky about this investigation.
- 12 August: A whistleblower complaint is filed with Michael Atkinson, the intelligence community's inspector general.
- 9 September: Atkinson informs House Intelligence Committee Chairman Adam Schiff (D-Cal.) about the whistleblower complaint, describing it as 'urgent' and 'credible'.
- 20 September: Media reports surface linking the whistleblower complaint to Ukraine. President Trump calls the reports 'fake news' and 'presidential harassment'.
- 24 September: House Speaker Nancy Pelosi (D-Cal.) announces that the House will begin a formal impeachment inquiry of the President.
- 25 September: The White House releases its version of a 'transcript' of the President's 25 July phone call.
- 22 October: In closed-door testimony to impeachment investigators in Congress, William B. Taylor, America's top diplomat in Ukraine called the situation created by the President 'a rancorous story about whistle-blowers, Mr Giuliani, side channels, quid pro quos, corruption and interference in elections'.

- 29 October 29: Lt.Col. Alexander Vindman told a closed-door House hearing how he was listening in to Trump's 25 July phone call and believed that what the President was asking of the Ukranian president 'would undermine US national security' and was improper. He was told by a top White House lawyer not to discuss his concerns with anyone outside the White House. He also said that some key details of the call were missing from the 'transcript' published by the White House.
- 31 October: House of Representatives voted (232–196) to formally approve the impeachment inquiry.
- 13 November: Public impeachment hearings commence in the House Intelligence Committee, lasting until 21 November.
- 3 December: House Intelligence Committee voted along party lines (13–9) to adopt the Intelligence Committee's Report and send it to the House Judiciary Committee.
- 4 December: House Judiciary Committee begins the process of drawing up articles of impeachment against President Trump.
- 10 December: House Judiciary Committee approves two articles of impeachment: Article I, Abuse of Power; Article II, Obstruction of Congress. Both are approved by the committee on party line votes (23–17).
- 18 December: the House of Representatives approves both articles of impeachment: Article I by 230-197; Article II by 229–198. Two Democrats voted 'no' on Article I and three voted 'no' on Article II. Independent (former Republican) member Justin Amash of Michigan voted 'yes' on both articles.

Analysis

So how significant is the President's impeachment, given that there seems to be no chance of the Senate removing him from office? It depends who you ask! President Trump and his supporters will say it is of no significance, because in their view the whole process was 'a witch hunt' and 'a hoax'. Meanwhile, the Democrats will claim it is of great significance and shows that the checks and balances of the Constitution are effective at calling to account a president who abuses his power. But maybe the political commentator Elizabeth Drew is nearer the mark when she wrote: 'The current proceedings have demonstrated just how fragile the Constitution's impeachment clause is [...] It's now clearer than ever that it doesn't work very well in the context of a very partisan political atmosphere.' If she is right, and if politics in Washington continues to be so polarised, this represents a serious weakness in the basic checks and balances of the Constitution. To put it simply, the only way to remove a president is through the ballot box.

It is also true to say that the concept of the 'imperial presidency' offers something for everyone. It means different things to different people at different times. This leads to two difficulties in using the term. First, presidents are not emperors. They are leaders, not rulers — which means that they are not really 'imperial' at all. Donald Trump may be a lot of things, but he is not a twenty-first-century version of Julius Caesar. Second, the concept of the 'imperial presidency' has come to be used by some as a term of disapproval — a term to attach to any presidency of which they do not approve. One really needs to avoid falling into this trap. It is also important to remember what Alexander Hamilton — one of the nation's Founding Fathers — wrote about the office of the president at the very outset in *Federalist 70*: 'Energy in the executive is a leading character in the definition of good government.' The question is: would Mr Hamilton regard President Trump as a purveyor of 'good government' or as a potential threat to the very system of limited and checked government that he helped to establish?

Comparison

The power of the individual at the head of the executive branch in the USA and the UK has long been contrasted, and UK prime ministers have faced questions about whether they are acting more like presidents.

- Both the US president and the UK prime minister command an impressive influence in being able to use the media as a tool of power. However, Trump has embraced social media, as Obama did with news sites such as Buzzfeed, as a way to wield power away from the scrutiny that more traditional news outlets allow. The UK prime minister has struggled more with this change, in part due to the culture of the UK public.
- Both the US and UK executives have seen increasingly similar challenges from a 'divided government'. While traditionally the UK prime minister would hold a substantial majority and the US president would fear losing one or both houses of Congress in the midterms, election results in the UK since 2010 have made the prime minister's position far more precarious. Both leaders are far from guaranteed support in their legislatures any more.
- Nonetheless, the US president can rely on a number of enumerated powers that are granted to him alone by the US Constitution. The UK prime minister, by comparison, remains *primus inter pares* (first among equals) and when they find themselves in a perilous political situation, they are far less able to respond with unchecked powers.

Summary

In this chapter we have covered the following issues:

- the background to the term 'imperial presidency' — who coined it and why
- the four main characteristics of the imperial presidency
- to what extent these four characteristics are evidenced in the presidency of Donald Trump
- a brief explanation of the impeachment process and a summary of the impeachment of President Trump
- some words of caution about the possible limitations and misuse of the term 'imperial presidency'

Further reading and research

A good follow-up to this chapter is the debate article in *Politics Review*, September 2018, Vol. 28, No. 1, 'Has Donald Trump restored the imperial presidency?' by Kay Moxon and Clare Stansfield.

The article referred to in Box 5.3 by Elizabeth Drew: 'The impeachment process is barely functioning', *New York Times*, 15 December 2019.

Chapter 6

Foreign policy

Exam success

Foreign policy is a policy area that is usually dominated by the US president. The Constitution gives the president the role of 'Commander in Chief of the Army and Navy of the United States' and, despite Congress's power to declare war, the presidency does seem to be able to exert significant control in this area. The best students will recognise that many of the checks that the Supreme Court and Congress have in this area often prove ineffective at preventing the president from acting. When considering if the president is an 'imperial president', it is not the lack of checks that is significant, but the lack of *effective* checks.

It is also crucial that students recognise that the presidency is not one man. The Constitution rests executive authority in one man, the president, but the presidency is a large and often unwieldy branch of government. It contains the Executive Office of the President, the cabinet and 15 executive departments, in addition to the agencies, commissions and corporations within its grasp. So when a department acts, it acts on behalf of, and under the authority of, the president.

Similarly, the best students will recognise that power over foreign policy waxes and wanes over time, both within and between presidencies. Control of the three branches of government, along with national and global circumstances, has a substantial impact on where power lies in this area. While Congress and the Supreme Court can act to try to limit presidential power, their role in foreign policy is almost always reactive — they can only act once the president has already done something. In this scenario, therefore, Congress and the Supreme Court are almost always in a weaker position than the president.

AQA	3.2.1.2	Congress: ■ the relationship of Congress to the executive branch of government ■ the structure, role and powers of the US Congress ■ debates concerning the functions, powers and effectiveness of Congress in legislation, oversight and the power of the purse
	3.2.1.3	Presidency: ■ sources of presidential power ■ difference between formal powers and informal powers ■ constraints on President's ability to exercise those powers

Edexcel	2.2.3	Congress: oversight
	3.1	The presidency: formal sources of presidential power as outlined in the US Constitution and their use
	3.3	The presidency: ■ relationships between the presidency and other branches ■ limitations on presidential power and why this varies between presidents
	3.4	Interpretations and debates of the US presidency: ■ the role and power of the president in foreign policy

Context

The US presidents of the twenty-first century have dealt with a number of unique and unprecedented foreign policy events — terrorist events, an increasing number of natural disasters and growing globalisation. President George W. Bush led the 'War on Terror' and President Obama led air strikes on Libya and Syria and signed both the Joint Comprehensive Plan of Action (JCPOA) with Iran and the Paris Climate Agreement. In 2016, the Republican Party not only won the White House with President Trump, they also won both houses of Congress. In the 2 years that followed, these two branches were also able to place two conservatives justices on the Supreme Court, making it more conservative leaning than it has been in the last few decades.

The foreign policy rhetoric of the Trump campaign emphasised the US relationship with Mexico and 'the wall', but since taking office President Trump has found himself embroiled in a range of foreign policy issues. Whether it is trade war with China, developing the relationship with North Korea, withdrawing from the JCPOA or threatening the captain of an Iranian oil tanker, the Trump administration has continued to show the strengths and weaknesses of the president's control over foreign policy.

The Iranian oil tanker incident

Background

The relationship between the USA and Iran has seen increasing tensions since President Trump withdrew the USA from the JCPOA in 2018. The JCPOA was an agreement between China, France, Russia, the United Kingdom, the United States, Germany and Iran that allowed limited nuclear action by Iran in exchange for reduced sanctions (see Box 6.2) from the other signatories. When this was signed in July 2015, it caused controversy in the US Congress, especially among Republicans, partly because the deal was not put to Congress despite its constitutional right to agree to — or ratify — all treaties. Instead, President Obama signed it as an executive agreement, limiting any power that Congress might have to influence the USA's role in the deal. Withdrawing from a treaty or a previous executive agreement does not require a president to obtain congressional consent,

so President Trump simply withdrew from the JCPOA in May 2018. There was little Congress could have done to prevent this action, even if it had wanted to.

Both in entering into, and leaving, the JCPOA, the power of the US presidency is demonstrated, as are the substantial limitations of the constitutional powers of Congress. After withdrawing from the agreement, President Trump's administration conducted a 'maximum pressure' campaign against Iran, which it suspects of supporting terrorism against the USA in the Middle East region. While the situation was already tense between the USA and Iran, an event in the Mediterranean Sea in the summer of 2019 threatened to push relations to breaking point, both with Iran and with the USA's European allies.

The events

A timeline of the main events is given in Box 6.1. An Iranian tanker, the *Adrian Darya 1*, carrying billions of dollars of oil, was seized by British authorities in Gibraltar in July 2019. It was suspected of carrying this oil to Syria in violation of EU sanctions. The USA was not interested in the destination of the oil, however, but in the ownership of the ship. It had imposed a series of sanctions against Iran in December 2018 after withdrawing from the JCPOA. These sanctions included a ban on the buying and selling of oil from Iran. The USA wanted to prevent the *Adrian Darya 1* being released from Gibraltar as it believed the sale of the oil would benefit the Iranian Revolutionary Guard and the Iranian government.

Box 6.1	Timeline of events
4 July 2019	Iranian tanker *Adrian Darya 1* is detained in Gibraltar by British authorities as it is suspected of transporting oil to Syria against EU sanctions.
15 August 2019	US Justice Department tries to block the release of the *Adrian Darya 1*, but the move is unsuccessful with Gibraltar saying the US sanctions on Iran are not enforceable in the EU. The *Adrian Darya 1* is released from Gibraltar after giving assurances its cargo was not destined for Syria, although Iran later denies making these assurances.
16 August 2019	US Justice Department issues a warrant to seize the tanker.
20 August 2019	US State Department warns EU countries not to offer harbour to the *Adrian Darya 1*.
26 August 2019	The US State Department contacts the captain of the *Adrian Darya 1*, offering him millions of dollars to pilot the vessel into waters where it can be seized by the USA.
6 September 2019	The *Adrian Darya 1* is sighted 2 miles off Syria.

In order to prevent the release of the Iranian tanker, two US executive departments became involved in trying to shape US foreign policy. Initially, the US Justice Department began court proceedings in Gibraltar to try to prevent the release of the tanker. When this failed, it issued a warrant which ordered any US law enforcement agency as well as any other authorised law enforcement agency to seize the *Adrian Darya 1* and her cargo. While both of these attempts were ultimately unsuccessful, they demonstrate the way in which the US presidency attempts to shape foreign policy through judicial means, relying on international relations with allies to enforce its will.

With this strategy failing, the USA stepped up international pressure in another way, through the State Department. Secretary of State Mike Pompeo announced that the *Adrian Darya 1* had been blacklisted and that any country offering assistance to the tanker risked facing sanctions from the USA.

Box 6.2   What are sanctions?

Sanctions are punishments placed by one country on another. They may be placed on a country because of an action it has taken or is threatening to take, or due to ideological differences. There are different types of sanctions, most commonly:

- trade/economic sanctions: banning imports from or exports to a country, including arms sales
- financial sanctions: freezing the financial assets of people from or related to a country
- smart sanctions: sanctions which target a small number of people, usually the elite, within a country

The aim of sanctions is to alter the behaviour of the country that is being sanctioned, after which sanctions would be lifted.

European countries were urged by Secretary Pompeo not to give any assistance to the *Adrian Darya 1* or to allow it to harbour in their countries, threatening 'heavy consequences' for anyone who did. In this way, the USA was relying on its importance as a political and trading ally to these EU countries and trying to shape their actions to support US foreign policy through such threats.

The US State Department further tried to achieve its foreign policy goals by offering the ship's captain millions of dollars to pilot the ship into waters where it could be seized by US officials. This offer is a part of the USA's 'maximum pressure' campaign on Iran. It creates international pressure to weaken Iranian finances, putting pressure on the country to stop enriching uranium and to stop supporting opposition groups to the USA in the Middle East region.

Analysis
It is no real surprise that these moves were driven by the presidency with little comment from Congress, as for much of the time that the crisis was developing, Congress was in recess. This raises considerable questions about Congress's

ability to oversee the presidential branch. Few of these actions are covered by enumerated powers, those explicitly given to the presidential branch in the Constitution. Equally, had Congress not been in recess, there is little it could have done to influence this situation. While Congress could perhaps have tried to use its legislative power, creating legislation is a hugely slow and laboured process, and legislation only has power within the borders of the USA.

The power of the presidency, however, is very clear. These are actions that were designed by the Trump administration to create pressure — pressure on US allies to fall in line with US policy, and pressure on those under US sanctions by attempting to limit the money to which their government has access. Frequently, these actions of the Justice and State Departments have been reported in the press as those of the 'Trump administration'. It is important, therefore, to recognise that while these may not be the actions of the President himself, they are actions committed by his branch of government and in his name, therefore supporting the power that this branch of government has over foreign policy. These actions are trying to change the behaviour of Iran to be in line with US ideals. Since sanctions were reinstated, the economic growth of Iran has fallen to −6% and the country has been producing over 1 million fewer barrels of oil each day.

While the president may be able to dominate foreign policy as compared to Congress or the Supreme Court, his power extends only as far as US borders. Beyond this, whilst the presidency can attempt to influence international situations, the president has little power over other sovereign nations and is reliant instead on the pressure his government can bring to bear on a region.

The trade war with China

Background

Another way in which foreign policy can be shaped is through tariffs. These are effectively extra taxes placed on imported products, usually to encourage citizens to buy products made in their own country rather than those made abroad. The impact on other countries is that their sales fall and the amount of money their government has therefore reduces. For President Trump, this was part of his campaign to 'Make America Great Again', working to strengthen the US economy and increase the number of jobs that were available for Americans. It was also in retaliation for Chinese companies allegedly stealing the intellectual property of US companies, through activities such as counterfeiting.

The events

Box 6.3 shows the principal events in the history of the USA's trade war with China.

Box 6.3 The trade war timeline

23 March 2018	President Trump's 25% tariffs on steel and aluminium go into effect.
2 April 2018	China imposes 25% tariffs on 128 US products.
3 April 2018	USA unveils plans for 25% tariffs on $50 billion of Chinese imports.
4 April 2018	China unveils plans for tariffs on $50 billion of US imports.
June 2018	Both China and the USA revise their list of products to face tariffs.
6 July 2018	First tariffs go into effect on $34 billion of imports by both China and the USA.
10 July 2018	USA unveils plans for 10% tariff on $200 billion of Chinese imports.
23 August 2018	Second phase of tariffs go into effect on $16 billion of imports by both China and the USA.
24 September 2018	Further tariffs go into effect on $200 billion of Chinese imports and $60 billion of US imports.
10 May 2019	US tariffs on $200 billion of Chinese imports increase from 10% to 25%.
1 August 2019	USA announces a further 10% tariff on $300 billion of Chinese imports. China retaliates with further tariffs on $25 billion of US imports.

The increasing tensions between these two countries, and the reported 'trade war' that has made headlines in the press, are a superb example of the power of the presidency. The initial investigation into Chinese intellectual property theft was carried out by the US trade representative. This is a cabinet role and therefore part of the executive branch. It is also the trade representative whom President Trump has instructed to raise tariffs as tensions have increased between the USA and China.

Equally, the escalating 'war' was briefly halted while the President attended the G7 summit, at which he and President Xi Jinping discussed the situation in which the two countries found themselves. In attending events like this, the President is acting as the head of state, the embodiment of the USA, and is able to act relatively free of congressional control in negotiating with other world leaders.

Analysis

Members of the House of Representatives and senators like Senator Pat Toomey (Republican-Pennsylvania) have criticised President Trump's approach, concerned that the impact of the tariffs has been to depress the US economy. However, there is little they could have done to prevent the escalation, especially given that concerns over Chinese business practices extend decades back before President Trump took office. The apparent deference shown by Congress could be seen as Congress giving its authority for President Trump to act in this manner,

but in reality there is little it could have done even if it had wanted to, given the hyper-partisan nature of the USA today.

Nonetheless, not everyone in Congress has sat idly by. President Trump's actions were carried out under the Trade Expansion Act. Some House members and senators, driven by veteran senator Chuck Grassley (Republican-Iowa), have suggested that a bill could be brought forward to attempt to limit the President's trade policies. According to Senator Grassley:

> It adds up to something pretty simple: Congress has delegated too much authority to the president of the United States... There's absolutely no constitutional crisis that this president or any other president has created. The constitutional crisis comes from the elected representatives of the people over the last 80 years making a dictator out of the presidency.

However, it has proved problematic to reconcile the competing interests in Congress to achieve the goals of Senator Grassley, and it has already taken a year to try to get the bill through Congress. Therefore, although it seems that Congress is unwilling simply to cede power to the presidency, it is limited in its ability to act quickly enough to have an impact on his foreign policy. In the year that this bill has been in Congress, the trade war with China has escalated dramatically; even if the bill is passed, it seems it will be rather too late to have any immediate impact.

Yemen

Background
The civil war in Yemen has been raging for years, at great cost to its citizens. In 2019, however, it proved to be a situation over which Congress was able to exert more power than it managed over either Iran or the tariff war with China. Saudi Arabia, supported by arms sales and intelligence from the USA, has been involved in the civil war, working to restore the former Yemeni government against the Iran-backed Houthi rebels.

The events
In 2019, US Congress intervened. In April 2019, it passed a bipartisan resolution invoking the 1970s War Powers Resolution and voting to end US involvement in the Yemeni war. However, this was met with a presidential veto. In July 2019, Congress then worked to pass a law that would have prevented President Trump from continuing arms sales to Saudi Arabia, which many feared could be used in the Yemen war. The bill passed both Houses of Congress but faced the same fate as the earlier resolution and was vetoed by President Trump. Congress was unable to find the votes to override this veto and therefore it remained in place.

Analysis
While on the surface this looks like a reiteration of the power of the presidency, both of these attempts were important rebukes to President Trump. The votes

made headlines around the world, and these two vetoes make up 40% of the vetoes currently issued by Donald Trump. That both were bipartisan votes suggests that he did not have the support or control over his own party and demonstrates Congress's willingness to stand up to the President in this policy area.

This is especially notable as it reflects the impact of the Democrats taking over the House of Representatives in the election of 2018 and of there being only a small Republican majority in the Senate. It is also notable for the fact that the War Powers Resolution of the 1970s has not so far been particularly influential in curbing presidential power, and its use here demonstrates Congress's willingness to find different routes to try to achieve this.

In addition to the bills regarding Yemen, Congress also passed another bill to prevent the President from going to war with Iran without seeking the approval of Congress. This further demonstrates Congress's willingness to challenge the president, but is also a sad reflection on the importance of the US Constitution. As Congress already holds the power to declare war, from Article I of the US Constitution, this bill should be superfluous. That Congress felt the need to pass it shows not only its unwillingness to let presidential power grow exponentially, but also the lack of power the US Constitution apparently has in restricting the power of the president as originally intended.

Comparison

In both the USA and the UK, foreign policy was an area of substantial controversy in 2019:

- As the USA has a directly elected president with his own mandate, he is far more able than the UK prime minister to take control of foreign policy. In the UK, the fact that the executive is drawn from the legislature, and the very small or non-existent majority since 2017, means that the legislature has been able to take greater control of foreign policy issues, notably Brexit.
- Both the USA and UK have cabinets as part of the executive branch, but the US presidency is not collective while the UK executive is. This means that cabinet members in the USA have greater freedom to act than their counterparts in the UK, who are bound by collective responsibility.
- Comparatively, both the US and UK cabinets saw substantial turnover in members in 2019 and both saw rebels against their executive. While the President saw the loss of the head of the Homeland Security and Justice Departments, the UK saw the loss of the Defence Secretary for leaks and numerous others over Brexit. There is therefore commonality in the fractious nature of the cabinet in both countries currently.

Summary

Foreign policy has traditionally been an area dominated by the presidency and 2019 was no exception:

- While Congress and the Supreme Court have previously stepped in and tried to shape policy in this area, they are rarely able to overturn it.
- The US Constitution offers other branches little power over foreign policy, being not only reactive but also hugely limited in their power. While Congress can approve a treaty — if it is lucky enough to be asked — it can do nothing to prevent a president from withdrawing from it.
- Congressional control over foreign policy therefore involves the exercise of pressure alongside the congressional 'power of the purse'. This is not an insignificant threat, but it is less prevalent when government is united.
- In foreign policy, the USA is viewed as one country rather than a collection of states; given this reality, it is always likely that the president will retain a greater degree of both power and influence in this area.
- The reality remains that, while Congress is increasingly willing to challenge the aggressive foreign policy of President Trump, its ability to have a substantive impact in this area appears limited by time, power and hyper-partisanship.

Further reading and research

- Research one of the following policies that President Trump has changed in his time in office and evaluate the power that this demonstrates: the North American Free Trade Agreement; the Trans-Pacific Partnership; the moving of the American Embassy to Jerusalem; the Paris Agreement.
- Create a chart showing the changes in President Trump's cabinet in his first term and why they happened. What does this suggest about where power lies in the executive branch?
- Read 'Trump's foreign policy moments' on the Council for Foreign Relations website (www.cfr.org). Create a graph showing how Trump's power has increased or decreased in this policy area between 2017 and 2020.
- Aiming for an A? Read 'How Congress and President shape US foreign policy' at www.europarl.europa.eu to expand your knowledge of the enumerated and implied powers of both of these branches in the US Constitution.

Chapter 7

Guns

Guns and the 2018 election

The issue of the right to own guns made numerous headlines in 2018, with political scientists looking at the contributions that groups such as the NRA made to the 2018 midterm election campaigns. The March for our Lives took place in March 2018, organised by the survivors of the MSD School shooting. It was notable for the speech made by survivor Emma González, who not only made an impassioned call for gun control, but named the 17 victims of the shooting before standing silent until 6 minutes and 20 seconds had elapsed – the time it took for the MSD shooting to take place.

The impacts of the MSD School shooting and subsequent protests were notable in their scale. Emma González and her peers were at the forefront of media headlines about gun control, and interest groups such as Everytown for Gun Control and Giffords began making significant strides in the funding they obtained and the ability this gave them to try to influence the 2018 midterms. This coincided with a decrease in spending from the NRA in this election cycle.

Why did NRA spending decrease in 2018?

In the face of such strident opposition, it seems counter-intuitive that NRA spending on the midterms was lower than it had previously been. In fact, some estimates claimed that the NRA spent as much as 90% less than in the previous midterm elections, spending $1.6 million in 2018 compared to $16 million in 2014, although this depends on exactly what is counted within these figures. The website OpenSecrets, which tracks money and lobbying in elections, suggests that the NRA was outspent by gun control groups, with the former spending $10 million and the latter spending $11 million. But was the money well spent by either side?

The results from the 2018 midterms did see some pro-gun rights incumbent House members lose their seats, such as in Virginia and Colorado. In fact, 27 members who supported gun rights lost their seats, while 6 members favouring gun control lost theirs. The statistical chance of an incumbent House member or senator losing their seat is so small that it is notable that gun control groups were able to unseat those whom they targeted. However, the Republicans retained their majority in the Senate, and the majority of senators remain pledged to block any gun control legislation that might be passed.

On the day of the midterms, the NRA tweeted: 'We get the judges, they get Pelosi.' This is a reference to its success in the appointment of Brett Kavanaugh to the Supreme Court. The NRA had campaigned heavily in favour of his appointment as a justice because of his record of protecting the rights of gun owners. Therefore this mocking tweet suggests that the NRA had other notable victories in 2018. Both the NRA and groups such as the Everytown for Gun Safety said they won 80% of the seats that they were targeting. So perhaps some of the spending decrease from the NRA can be explained by a confidence of success in the seats that it was targeting. However, the headlines made by prominent mass shootings saw its membership numbers fall, which affected the amount of money the NRA received and led to the organisation being in deficit in terms of its income and outgoings for the second year in a row. In addition, in the aftermath of the MSD School shootings, 20 major American companies such as United and Delta airlines severed their ties with the NRA in a major blow to its finances and reputation.

Nonetheless, despite a spending drop, the NRA does not find itself in a particularly poor position in terms of congressional support for its goals. It lost some seats in terms of those supporting gun rights but is far from facing imminent defeat in Congress. Of greater concern perhaps will be the financial situation that it finds itself in as the 2020 election approaches.

The growth in gun control contributions

Gun control groups, however, had notable success in 2018. The NRA annually rates each member of Congress, giving them a grade from A+ to F depending on their support for gun rights. The Giffords group, co-founded by Congresswomen Gabrielle Giffords, who was shot in the head in 2011, targeted four incumbents with an A-grade rating from the NRA. Spending more than $5 million in the midterms, the group helped to unseat all four incumbents. In fact, 95 candidates backed by the Giffords group won seats in the midterms, while 32 who had been backed by the NRA lost their seats.

In all cases, however, the effect of money targeted at a seat varied greatly between different districts, as Table 7.1 shows.

Table 7.1 NRA and gun control group contributions in selected districts, 2018 midterms

	NRA contributions to the Republican candidate ($)	Gun control group contributions to the Democratic candidate ($)	Winner
Virginia, District 10	12,158	997,825	Democrat
North Carolina, District 13	208,965	2,861	Republican
Florida, District 25	3,000	207,500	Republican
Minnesota, District 8	200,977	–	Republican
New York, District 22	93,179	3,861	Democrat
Kansas, District 2	72,692	–	Republican
Virginia, District 5	65,490	–	Republican
Iowa, District 3	59,590	861	Democrat

Results in just these few districts demonstrate that amount spent did not always correlate to outcome, highlighting that other factors were at play in each of these district elections. As ever when it comes to pressure groups, it is hugely important to recognise that money spent does not always equate to a certain outcome. While pressure groups with the most money are able to spend more, it does not necessarily follow that they will get what they want.

Guns in 2019 — a change of mood?

Gun violence in 2019

In the first part of 2019 alone, the statistics of gun violence were surprising to many (see Table 7.2). These statistics, however, were on course to match previous years, in which there were an average of 50,000–60,000 incidents annually.

Table 7.2 Gun violence, January–August 2019

Total number of gun incidents	38,742
Number of gun deaths	10,225
Number of gun injuries	20,444
Mass shootings	292
Unintentional shootings	1,149

Source: The Gun Violence Archive, January–August 2019

Box 7.1   Selected mass shootings in 2019

Aurora, Illnois (February): 5 people killed

Virginia Beach, Virginia (May): 12 people killed

Dayton, Ohio (August): 10 people killed

El Paso, Texas (August): 22 people killed

Midland-Odessa, Texas (August): 8 people killed

Jersey City, New Jersey (December): 6 people killed

Given this situation, it is difficult to understand why there would be any difference in the chances of achieving gun control. However, in Congress, across businesses, from lobbying groups and in US public opinion more generally, there does seem to be an increasing momentum for gun control, perhaps driven by some of the success for gun control groups in the 2018 midterms.

Legislation

The Democrats having taken control of the House of Representatives, 2019 saw gun control legislation passed very early on in the congressional session. The Bipartisan Background Checks Act passed the House by 240 to 190, mostly along party lines with Democrats voting for and Republicans voting against. However, President Trump has said that, should this bill make its way to him, he would veto it, and it has yet even to pass the Senate. Therefore, while the momentum of the last year or so may be high on gun control, the actual outcome is rather more muted.

After the El Paso shooting in Texas in the summer of 2019, however, when 22 people were killed, President Trump came out in favour of limited gun control reform, known as 'red-flag' laws. These laws allow family members or law enforcement officials to petition the state for a temporary ban on gun ownership for those who may present a danger to themselves or to others. President Trump stated:

> We must make sure that those judged to pose a grave risk to public safety do not have access to firearms, and that if they do, those firearms can be taken through rapid due process. That is why I have called for red-flag laws, also known as extreme-risk protection orders.

Seventeen states already have 'red-flag' laws, and the idea received bipartisan support from a range of notable House members and senators. The NRA has expressed some support for the measure, but when it has actually come to legislation the NRA has worked against such bills, citing concerns over people unduly losing their Second Amendment rights. Nonetheless, this is the closest the US Congress has come to being in agreement on passing gun control since the banning of bump stocks after the Las Vegas shooting in 2017. Even this legislation was very limited, preventing semi-automatic weapons being convertible to fully automatic weapons, rather than preventing the sale of assault-style rifles.

President Trump has supported some forms of gun control after mass shootings before, only for little actually to come of it. After the MSD School shooting he said, 'Take the guns first, go through due process second', much to the concern of gun rights activists. Once the furore had died down, however, such control was not forthcoming, either from the President or from Congress with few willing to challenge the cultural expectation of gun ownership. Therefore, while there did seem to have been a shift in the public mood in 2019, whether it will last long enough to result in meaningful change, especially in an election year, remains to be seen.

Corporations

Equally, corporations in the USA have begun taking action. Walmart decided to stop selling ammunition for assault rifles and to stop customers carrying weapons openly in its stores. The El Paso massacre took place in a Walmart. Just days before that shooting, two Walmart workers were killed by another Walmart worker in Mississippi. In Missouri, in the same month, a man was arrested after walking into a Walmart wearing body armour and carrying a loaded weapon, purportedly to 'test' the protection of his Second Amendment rights. After Walmart's decision, other US retailers such as Walgreens and CVS followed suit. It seems, therefore, that while the US government may be slow to act, the momentum created by groups such as Everytown for Gun Safety and headlines made by mass shootings are not only denting NRA coffers, but also impacting change in other non-legislative ways.

The Supreme Court takes a gun control case

Until 2019 the Supreme Court had not heard a gun control case since 2010 in the case of *Chicago* v *Macdonald*. This case found the states could not infringe upon a citizen's right to carry weapons for self-defence. In its ruling, however, one of the Court's most conservative justices, Antonin Scalia, commented: 'Like most rights, the Second Amendment right is not unlimited. It is not a right to keep and carry any weapons whatsoever in any manner whatsoever and for whatever purpose.' Since then, the Supreme Court has largely shied away from gun control cases. While the Supreme Court does not comment on why this is the case, in 2018 Justice Clarence Thomas commented that 'The right to keep and bear arms is apparently this Court's constitutional orphan', suggesting perhaps that it is not an accidental occurrence.

It is certainly not as if the Supreme Court has been without the opportunity, having had eight cases referred to it in recent years. However, the Supreme Court chooses from around 8,000 cases annually, and it has largely chosen to ignore gun control cases. But with six of the ten deadliest mass shootings in US history occurring in the last 10 years, perhaps the Court's hand has now been forced and it took up two gun rights cases in 2019.

The Court agreed in January 2019 to consider the case of *New York State Rifle & Pistol Association Inc.* v *City of New York*. This case concerns the state regulation in New York City which prevents gun owners from transporting weapons other than to the seven gun ranges within the city limits; gun owners cannot transport their weapons outside of the city limits. As a state, New York has one of the strictest laws on guns in the USA. Gun rights groups and the Justice Department hope the Supreme Court will rule against New York in the case and therefore expand the limits of the Second Amendment. Notably, it is the first gun rights case heard since the newly appointed conservative justices took their seats on the Court.

In the summer of 2019, New York City changed the laws surrounding the transportation of weapons, apparently in the hope that the Supreme Court would no longer feel the need to hear the case in the 2019–20 session. However, as yet the case remains on the docket, although the Court could now remove it if it wishes. Its willingness to take up the case can perhaps be attributed in part to the high-profile nature of the gun control debate in 2019. However, chances that this ruling would result in gun control seem slim. Justice Anthony Kennedy was part of the five-justice majority in the 2008 case of *Heller* v *District of Columbia*. His replacement, Justice Brett Kavanaugh, commented on a case he heard in 2011:

> It follows from Heller's protection of semi-automatic handguns that semi-automatic rifles are also **constitutionally** protected and that D.C.'s ban on them is unconstitutional.

Justice Kavanaugh was endorsed by the NRA when he was nominated to the Supreme Court by President Trump. If the Court chooses to hear the case, it will certainly give a clear indication as to its leanings and serve to demonstrate the importance – or not – of ideology in the Court's rulings. Despite a more general mood of optimism about gun control in the USA, however, the Supreme Court seems much more likely to extend gun rights in the coming year, if it hears the case at all.

The Supreme Court and Sandy Hook

As well as taking up the New York City case, the Supreme Court found itself asked to intervene in a second notable gun control case in 2019, regarding the 2012 Sandy Hook massacre in which 20 elementary school children and six staff were killed. In March 2019, the Connecticut Supreme Court reinstated a wrongful death lawsuit that was brought against Remington, the makers of the AR-15 Bushmaster assault weapon that was used in the massacre. The claim was allowed as the Connecticut Supreme Court decided the manufacturer had been irresponsible in its marketing for the rifle. In November 2019 the Supreme Court refused to hear an appeal from the Remington Arms company, allowing the case to continue and suggesting a change in the mood surrounding guns in 2019.

The 2020 presidential race

The issue of gun control has been made a key issue so far in the invisible primary for the 2020 Democratic nomination. No fewer than five of the key contenders have co-sponsored a bill banning assault weapons — Kamala Harris, Cory Booker, Kirsten Gillibrand, Amy Klobuchar, Bernie Sanders, and Elizabeth Warren. There equally seems to be a reasonable amount of common support among Democratic candidates for universal background checks and an assault weapons ban as well as some support for a weapons registry. Regardless of any policy pledges made during these campaigns, however, should any of these candidates win the presidential election, they would need to work with Congress to pass such laws. President Obama failed to get any meaningful gun control legislation passed in the wake of the Sandy Hook massacre, and these candidates would need the apparent shift in public mood both to persist and to be reflected in those elected to Congress in 2020.

Summary

Gun control in the USA remains an issue of huge controversy, despite general agreement that a level of control, not outright bans, is increasingly a necessity:

- With interest group spending on the side of gun control increasing, the National Rifle Association seems to face a real challenge to its rhetoric for the first time in decades.
- The political reality is that national legislation on gun control still seems a distant dream, and the progress being made remains piecemeal.
- Despite the vast amounts of money that interest groups spend to achieve their goals, factors such as the culture of the USA, the strength of the US Constitution, and the polarisation of opinion mean that too often a compromise seems out of reach.
- Politicians who have 'reached across the aisle' have found themselves marginalised or the target of negative campaigning, such as Democratic Senator Joe Manchin who was the target of both the NRA and President Trump's vitriol in the 2018 midterms.
- Despite the headlines, implementing gun control in a country of 400 million guns requires a great deal more political will than is currently evident, even with the changing mood of 2019.

Further reading and research

- Read 'US gun laws: Why it won't follow New Zealand's lead' (www.bbc.co.uk) and rank the factors that make gun control unlikely in order of importance, explaining why you put them in that order.
- Research the laws on gun control in three different states using https://lawcenter.giffords.org/scorecard/ to support your examples of federalism.
- Using www.opensecrets.org, research the amount of money being spent by pro-gun and gun control groups in 2019–20.
- Aiming for an A? Using www.opensecrets.org, go to the NRA page and click on 'lobbying'. Click on any one of the bills on which it has lobbied, and research what its objections were and how much it spent lobbying on that issue.

Chapter 8

What did the Supreme Court decide in 2018–19?

Exam success

The role of the US Supreme Court in the political sphere has a long history. However, the Constitution does not give it the power it appears to have today. Students should recognise that the Court's power comes from the two key cases of *Marbury* v *Madison* (1803) and *Fletcher* v *Peck* (1810), which means that today it effectively has the final say over the constitutionality of state and federal law as well as of executive branch actions. The best students, however, will recognise the limitations of such decisions. The Court can only hear around 80 cases a year, and relies on federal and state governments to enforce its rulings. There have been numerous cases even in recent history where such support has not been forthcoming for the Court.

Equally, the best students will recognise the threat that the Supreme Court represents to both the president and Congress. Sometimes, it is not the Court's action which is important, but the potential of its action. A president or Congress may shape their law knowing that the Supreme Court has the power to strike it down if it strays from the spirit of the US Constitution. This threat should not be underestimated and the best students will recognise that sometimes inaction and potential action are just as important as deciding to hear and rule upon a case.

AQA	3.2.1.1	US Constitution: protection of civil liberties and rights under the US Constitution, Bill of Rights, and Supreme Court rulings
	3.2.1.4	US Supreme Court: Supreme Court as protector of citizens' rights
	3.2.1.7	Pressure groups: methods, tactics and debates about their power
Edexcel	4	US Supreme Court and civil rights — nature and role of the Supreme Court and the protection of rights
	5.3	Interest groups in the USA: their significance, resources, tactics and debates about their impact on democracy

Context

The United States Supreme Court sits above the federal judiciary. It is composed of nine justices — one chief justice (currently John Roberts) and eight associate justices. They are appointed by the president, subject to confirmation by the Senate. They serve for life. The current members of the Court were appointed by George H. W. Bush (Thomas), Bill Clinton (Ginsburg and Breyer), George W. Bush (Roberts and Alito), Barack Obama (Sotomayor and Kagan) and Trump (Gorsuch and Kavanaugh).

The Court's significance comes from its power of judicial review, by which it can declare Acts of Congress or of the state legislatures, as well as actions of the federal or state executives — including the president — unconstitutional. Through this power, the Supreme Court acts as the arbiter and umpire of the Constitution, deciding whether laws or actions are compatible with it.

Supreme Court justices come to cases holding different judicial philosophies. Broadly, there are two different groups of justices based on their judicial philosophies: strict constructionists and loose constructionists. Strict constructionists tend to be conservative in outlook and interpret the Constitution in a strict or literal fashion, trying to mirror the original intent of the framers. They tend to be those appointed by Republican presidents. Loose constructionists tend to be liberal in outlook and see the Constitution as a living document, the meaning of which can change as America changes. They tend to be appointed by Democratic presidents.

The Court in 2018–19

At the end of the previous term, Justice Anthony Kennedy had retired and Brett Kavanaugh had been confirmed as his replacement (see *US Politics Annual Update 2019*, Chapter 9). It is often said that when a new justice joins the Court, it is not just a matter of a new justice, it is a new court. The balance of the Court changes. New alignments have to be formed. And, as we shall see, that was certainly true of this term. For years, Kennedy had played the 'centrist', the 'swing' justice sometimes joining the Court's liberal quartet to give them a majority; at other times joining the Court's conservative quartet to give them a majority. Indeed, in many of the landmark decisions, if you knew which way Justice Kennedy was going to decide, you knew which was going to be the winning side. Kennedy was invariably on that winning side. So Court watchers were waiting to see how the new Court would gel. For that reason, the 2018–19 term was one of special interest.

Of the 72 decisions handed down by the Court in this term — in itself pretty much par for the course — we shall consider six dealing with a number of different parts of the Constitution and raising issues in a number of different areas of policy and constitutional law (see Table 8.1).

Table 8.1 Selected Supreme Court decisions, 2018–19 term

Case	Concerning	Decision
The American Legion v *American Humanist Society*	Freedom of religion: separation of church and state	7–2
Bucklew v *Precythe*	Death penalty	5–4
Flowers v *Mississippi*	Rights of racial minorities	7–2
Lamone v *Benisek* and *Rucho* v *Common Cause*	Political gerrymandering	5–4
Department of Commerce v *New York*	Citizenship question on 2020 census	5–4

The First Amendment

The First Amendment begins thus: 'Congress shall make no law respecting an establishment of religion... . This is known as the establishment clause and was the focus for the case of *The American Legion* v *American Humanist Society*. The case revolved around a 40-foot cross which forms a First World War memorial in Bladensburg, Maryland. When it was constructed back in the 1920s, the construction was privately paid for and stood on private land. But in 1961 the land was passed to a state-run agency, meaning that the cross now stood on publicly owned land. Since that date, the state of Maryland has spent around $117,000 on the upkeep and repair of the memorial site. This led to the American Humanist Society — an atheist advocacy group — filing a lawsuit claiming that the use of state taxpayers' money to pay for the upkeep and repair of the site, including a Christian cross, violated the establishment clause of the First Amendment.

In the federal trial court, the judges found in favour of the state-run agency but the federal appeal court reversed that decision, agreeing with the American Humanist Society that the cross — positioned on public land and its upkeep paid for by taxpayers — violated the First Amendment. But the Supreme Court reversed the appeal court decision. Writing for the seven-member majority, Justice Samuel Alito stated that the monument did not primarily convey a religious message. The cross merely reflected the way fallen soldiers' graves were marked at that time in the nation's history. He added:

> That the cross originated as a Christian symbol and retains that meaning in many contexts does not change the fact that the symbol took on an added secular meaning when used in World War 1 memorials.

Alito also drew on the recent fire at Notre Dame Cathedral in Paris, noting:

> Although the French Republic rigorously enforces a secular public square, the cathedral remains a symbol of national importance to the religious and nonreligious alike. Notre Dame is fundamentally a place of worship and retains great religious importance, but its meaning has broadened. For many, it is now inextricably linked with the very idea of Paris and France.

But Justice Ginsburg joined by Justice Sotomayor disagreed. They felt that the Constitution was being violated. Justice Ginsburg wrote in her dissent:

> The cross is the foremost symbol of the Christian faith, embodying the central claim of Christianity: that the Son of God died on the cross, that he rose from the dead and that his death and resurrection offer the possibility of eternal life. The cross is not emblematic of any other faith.

The Court's decision found favour with President Trump, whose administration had argued for the cross's retention.

The Eighth Amendment

The Eighth Amendment forbids 'cruel and unusual punishments' from being inflicted. (The word 'unusual' would today be better understood as 'arbitrary'.) It is this amendment around which contemporary debate regarding the death penalty centres. The Court has handed down a number of death penalty judgements in the past two decades and it handed down another in this term.

In *Bucklew* v *Precythe*, the Court ruled (5–4) that a Missouri death-row inmate could be executed by lethal injection without infringement of his Eighth Amendment rights. Russell Bucklew was convicted of the 1996 slaying of his former girlfriend's lover. Bucklew had claimed that a rare physical condition would lead to a longer and more tortuous death than is usual by lethal injection, and would therefore infringe his constitutional rights. The five-justice majority consisted of Chief Justice Roberts joining with the Court's four conservative justices (see Table 8.2).

Table 8.2 Make-up of the Supreme Court by ideological position, 2018–19

Liberal wing	Swing justice	Conservative wing
Ruth Bader Ginsburg	John Roberts	Clarence Thomas
Sonia Sotomayor		Samuel Alito
Stephen Breyer		Neil Gorsuch
Elena Kagan		Brett Kavanaugh

Racial equality

Engraved over the front portico of the United States Supreme Court building in Washington DC are the words 'Equal Justice Under Law'. The phrase itself is not in the Constitution but is based on a phrase from the Fourteenth Amendment (1865) which forbids states from denying 'to any person within its jurisdiction the equal protection of the law'. In the case of *Flowers* v *Mississippi*, the Supreme Court ruled (7–2) that excluding black jurors from a criminal trial jury violated the Constitution. Writing for the Court's majority, Justice Brett Kavanaugh – the Court's newest member – stated: 'Equal justice under law requires a criminal trial free of racial discrimination in the jury selection process'. Justices Clarence Thomas and Neil Gorsuch dissented in this case. So here was a landmark decision of the Court in which the two Trump appointees were on different sides of the argument, and which suggested that, of the two, Gorsuch is the more ideologically conservative.

Curtis Flowers, a black man, was charged with the murder of four people in a furniture store back in 1996, a charge which Flowers has always denied. He has so far sat through six trials at which a white prosecutor, Doug Evans, has done his best to keep black people off the jury. In its 2019 decision, the Court concentrated on Mr Evans' professional record. In Flowers' first four trials — between 1997 and 2007 — Evans used all 36 juror challenges that he was allowed to keep 36 black potential jurors off the panels. Three of those trials ended in Mr Flowers' conviction, but all were overturned on appeal. The fourth was declared a mistrial, as was the fifth trial in 2008. For the sixth trial — the one in question in this case — the jury constituted 11 white members and one black member. But Evans objected to five other prospective jurors who were black. What was more significant was that, while Evans asked the 11 white jurors an average of one question each, he asked the six black prospective jurors an average of 29 questions each. Justice Kavanaugh — and six other justices — saw that pattern as problematic. Kavanaugh wrote for the majority:

> One can slice and dice the statistics and come up with all sorts of ways to compare the state's questioning of the accepted white jurors. But any meaningful comparison yields the same basic assessment: The state spent far more time questioning the black prospective jurors than the accepted white jurors.

Evans said that he had acceptable reasons for rejecting these black prospective jurors, including that they knew witnesses or members of Mr Flowers' family, had been sued by the furniture store where the murders took place, had doubts about the use of the death penalty, or had turned up late for jury selection. Kavanaugh rejected these reasons because either they were factually inaccurate or Evans had not pursued similar lines of investigation and questioning for the white jurors he accepted. On that basis, the Court agreed that Mr Flowers' constitutional rights had been infringed.

Political gerrymandering

We have left the best till last — and so did the Supreme Court, announcing its decisions in the gerrymandering and census cases on the Court's final morning. They were both 5–4 decisions. In the first, Chief Justice Roberts joined the Court's conservative quartet to give them the majority, while in the second he joined the Court's liberal quartet to put them on top. You can therefore use these two decisions in your essays to show how — given the new make-up of the Court following the retirement of Justice Kennedy — Roberts has become the new 'swing justice'. The Supreme Court now truly is the Roberts Court.

Terminology

First, some terminology. What is gerrymandering? It is the drawing of district (constituency) boundaries resulting in constituencies of odd and unnatural shapes to the political advantage of one party. After every 10-yearly census — in the zero-numbered years — district boundaries for the US House of Representatives and state legislatures have to be redrawn in order to create districts of roughly equal population. When, after the 1810 census, the Massachusetts legislature redrew the state senate lines, it created one district that was so odd in its shape, it was drawn by a cartoonist to represent a salamander — an amphibious, lizard-like creature. As the boundaries had been agreed to by the state governor, Elbridge Gerry, the process was given the name 'gerrymander'.

The Court's decision

In two cases decided together — *Lamone* v *Benisek* and *Rucho* v *Common Cause* — the Supreme Court decided (5–4) that the drawing of electoral boundaries falls outside the jurisdiction of the federal courts. Chief Justice Roberts, writing for the five-member majority — in which he was joined by the Court's conservative quartet — stated that the framers of the Constitution knew that politics would play a role in the drawing of electoral districts when they gave the task to the state legislatures. In the opinion of the Court's majority, federal judges were therefore not entitled to second-guess the state legislators' decisions. 'We conclude,' wrote the Chief Justice, 'that partisan gerrymandering claims present political questions beyond the reach of the federal courts.'

Importance of the decision

Why is this so important? For two reasons. First, the next national census will be conducted in 2020 and therefore new electoral maps will be drawn before the midterm elections for the House of Representatives in 2022. Second, it is widely believed that the most prominent examples of gerrymandering are likely to occur in states controlled by the Republicans, such as North Carolina and Ohio. Democrats were therefore especially disappointed by the Court's ruling. Currently, 10 of North Carolina's 13 House members are Republicans, as are 12 of Ohio's 16 House members.

For the minority, Justice Kagan wrote: 'The practices [of gerrymandering] in these cases imperil our system of government. Part of the Court's role in that system is to defend its foundations. None is more important than free and fair elections.'

Executive power

A topic that has become centre-stage for debate since Donald Trump entered the White House is that of executive power. Addressing a conservative student conference in Washington DC in July 2019, the President claimed — not for the first time: 'Then I have Article II, where I have the right to do whatever I want as president.' Law professor William C. Banks responded, calling Trump's remarks an affront 'to basic points that every child learns in civics classes'. Banks added: 'He's not a monarch, he's a chief executive and he's bound to uphold the rule of law.'

In the case of *United States Department of Commerce* v *New York*, the Court ruled (5–4) that Secretary of Commerce Wilbur Ross could not insert a question about citizenship into the 2020 census questionnaire. Although the case was seen as one concerning presidential and executive power, the part of the Constitution which was the focus of this case was the phrase in Article I, Section 2 that requires an 'actual enumeration' of each state every 10 years for the purpose of reallocating seats in the House of Representatives. The fear among opponents of the Trump administration's push to include a citizenship question in the 2020 census was that this would lead to a significant undercount of non-white people, to the political advantage of the Republican Party (see Box 8.1). So, for example, the American Civil Liberties Union (ACLU) claims that a census form with a citizenship question would frighten noncitizens from participating in the census, whether they are in the country legally or not. And an undercount of minority-race noncitizens would have the effect of diverting federal money and political power away from states and cities where larger numbers of such people live, and into the hands of rural areas, favouring the Republican Party.

Box 8.1   **Why is the citizenship question important?**

When it was first suggested that the Trump administration would try to insert a citizenship question into the 2020 census, the Census Bureau warned that it could scare off many immigrants from participating and therefore from being counted. For a century and a half now, each state's share of seats in the US House of Representatives has depended on the number living there as counted in the 10-yearly census.

But research published by the *Washington Post* (15 August 2019) found that, if undocumented immigrant numbers were removed from each state's population, this would result in, for example, California losing two House seats, New Jersey losing one House seat but Montana gaining one House seat. That is a scenario which clearly plays to the advantage of the Republican Party.

Commerce Secretary Ross had justified his inclusion of the citizenship question by saying that it was to enable his department to monitor compliance with the Voting Rights Act. But the justices disagreed. In his majority opinion, the Chief Justice wrote that the evidence showed that 'the Voting Rights Act played an insignificant role in the decision-making process'. Indeed, the Chief Justice virtually called Commerce Secretary Ross a liar (see Box 8.2).

Box 8.2   **Extract from Chief Justice Roberts' majority opinion in the *Department of Commerce* case**

The Secretary [of Commerce] was determined to reinstate a citizenship question from the time he entered office; instructed his staff to make it happen; waited while Commerce officials explored whether another agency would request census-based citizenship data; subsequently contacted the Attorney General himself to ask if [the] Department of Justice would make the request; and adopted the Voting Rights Act rationale late in the process. Altogether, the evidence tells a story that does not match the explanation the Secretary gave for his decision.

The four-member minority were indignant. Writing for the conservative quartet, Justice Alito remarked: 'To put the point bluntly, the federal judiciary has no authority to stick its nose into the question whether it is good policy to include a citizenship question on the census or whether the reasons given by Secretary Ross for that decision were his only reasons or his real reasons.' It was evident that Justice Alito was perfectly content to give the executive branch a very broad granting of unchecked power.

Comparison

The roles of the Supreme Courts in the US and UK are markedly different due to the location of sovereignty. However, with events in the UK in 2019, the UK Supreme Court seems ever more like its counterpart in the USA:

- Both the US and UK Supreme Courts have challenged the executive branches of their respective systems. In ruling that the prorogation of Parliament was unlawful, and having that rule adhered to, the UK Supreme Court demonstrated a power similar to that held by the US Supreme Court. In this way, both courts arguably have a political role. Note, however, that the UK Supreme Court cannot declare an Act of Parliament unconstitutional.
- The UK Supreme Court remains more apolitical than the US court due to the way in which justices are appointed. However, following the 2019 ruling on prorogation, there were discussions about whether this new role of the UK Supreme Court warranted an appointment process similar to that of the US Supreme Court.
- The role of the UK Supreme Court is still evolving, and is far from accepted within the UK political system. In contrast, the US Supreme Court took its most important power of judicial review in 1803 (over federal issues) and 1810 (over state issues) and therefore its power is both well understood and accepted.

Summary

In this chapter we have seen that the Supreme Court in its 2018–19 term:

- put limits on the separation of church and state
- declined to add further limitations on the use of the death penalty
- upheld the right of equality under the law for racial minorities in the selection of juries
- declined to become involved in the matter of the political gerrymandering of electoral districts
- restricted executive power in the case of the Trump administration's proposed citizenship question in the 2020 census

These decisions showed that:

- The Supreme Court's power of judicial review gives the Court great importance in a wide range of policy areas.
- Chief Justice John Roberts appears to be the new 'swing justice' in the nine-member Court following the retirement of Justice Anthony Kennedy.

- The two Trump appointees on the Court — Neil Gorsuch and Brett Kavanaugh — will not always be in agreement.
- Whereas some landmark decisions found favour with the President and his administration, others went against them.

Further reading and research

The following websites will enable you to follow the work of the Supreme Court. The Court sits between October and June, but many of the most important decisions are not announced until June — sometimes after you will have sat your examination. But it is worth checking one or two of these sites just before your exam to see if there is anything that has just been announced by the Court that you might be able to include in an exam essay.

- Robert Barnes is the *Washington Post*'s main writer on Supreme Court matters. Type 'Robert Barnes Washington Post' into a search engine to find his articles.
- Adam Liptak is the *New York Times'* main writer on the Supreme Court. Search for his articles on **www.nytimes.com**.
- **www.scotus.blog** is the Supreme Court's official blog and is full of details on the work of the Court, including statistics and videos.

Chapter 9

The Supreme Court: overview of the 2018–19 term

Exam success and Context

See the beginning of Chapter 8.

In Chapter 8 we analysed six significant decisions handed down by the Supreme Court in its term which began in October 2018 and ended in June 2019. But these were only six of the 72 decisions handed down by the Court during this term. As Table 9.1 shows, the number of cases that the Supreme Court has heard in recent years has varied little from year to year, but it is somewhat down on the average number of cases decided during the period when William Rehnquist was chief justice (1986–2005).

Of the 72 decisions made in the 2018–19 term, the vast majority (81%) were appealed from the federal appellate courts, with just 15% coming from the state appellate courts. Three were appealed from the court for the District of Columbia.

How united?

In terms of court unity, this term was almost identical to the previous term with 39% of decisions being unanimous while 28% split the Court by 5 votes to 4. As can be seen in Table 9.1, this means that the Court has settled back to normality after the unusual unanimity scores between 2015 and 2017 — at this time, the Court was often sitting with only eight members after the Senate refused to fill the vacancy created by the death of Justice Antonin Scalia in early 2016.

Table 9.1 Total, unanimous and 5–4 decisions, 2013–19

Term:	2013–14	2014–15	2015–16	2016–17	2017–18	2018–19
Number of decisions	72	75	76	69	71	72
% which were unanimous	65	40	50	59	39	39
% which were 5–4 decisions	14	26	5	10	27	28

Those 5–4 decisions

The decisions that often attract the most media interest are those that split the Court down the middle with five justices deciding one way and four deciding the other. Analysts then look to see which justices are in the majority and minority groupings, which justices are most frequently in the majority in such decisions, and whether or not there is any discernible trend in terms of conservative and liberal groupings in such decisions.

There were 20 5–4 decisions in the 2018–19 term, although Justice Brett Kavanaugh participated in only 18 of these. This was because Kavanaugh had been involved in the other two cases before they – and he – arrived at the Supreme Court, meaning that he had to recuse himself from the Supreme Court's decision. Table 9.2 shows that the frequency with which each justice was in the majority in 5–4 decisions was fairly equable. The justice most frequently in the majority was Trump appointee Neil Gorsuch, who was in the majority in 13 out of the 20 such cases. At the bottom of the table were the two Obama-nominated justices – Sonia Sotomayor and Elena Kagan – but they were in the majority in 10 of the decisions. This is very different from the previous term when, out of 19 5–4 decisions, Chief Justice Roberts had been in the majority in 17 of them, while Justice Kagan was in the majority in just 3. What this suggests is that in the 2018–19 term, the 5–4 decisions were made much less along ideological lines – conservatives and liberals – than in the previous year.

Table 9.2 Frequency in the majority in 5–4 decisions, 2018–19

Justice	Frequency in majority in 5–4 decisions (out of 20)
Neil Gorsuch	13
Brett Kavanaugh	11
Clarence Thomas	11
John Roberts	11
Samuel Alito	11
Ruth Bader Ginsburg	11
Stephen Breyer	11
Sonia Sotomayor	10
Elena Kagan	10

This is backed up by the data presented in Figure 9.1. This compares the percentage of times that Chief Justice Roberts and Justice Stephen Breyer have been in the majority in 5–4 decisions over the past nine terms. In decisions made along ideological lines, Roberts would tend to group with the conservatives while Breyer would group with the liberals. Whereas in 2017–18 Roberts was in the majority in 89% of 5–4 decisions and Breyer in only 21%, in the most recent term their respective percentages – 55% and 50% – were much more similar.

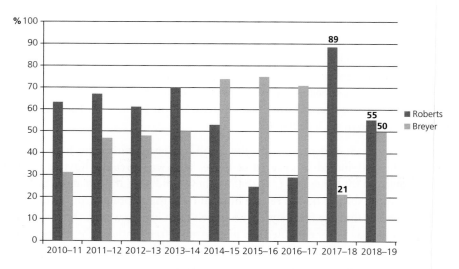

Figure 9.1 Percentage of times in the majority on 5–4 decisions, 2010–19: Roberts and Breyer compared

The 2018–19 term also saw a return to normality in the frequency with which the conservatives on the Court were in the majority in 5–4 decisions. This is shown by the data in Figure 9.2. We talked in Chapter 8 about the Court's current ideological make-up (see Table 8.2). So when we say that 'the conservatives' were in the majority in 35% of 5–4 decisions in 2018–19, we mean that justices Thomas, Alito, Gorsuch and Kavanaugh were joined by Chief Justice Roberts to form the majority in these seven decisions. Two of these were decisions that we looked at in Chapter 8 — on the death penalty and gerrymandering. In only two decisions did Roberts join the liberal quartet of justices Ginsburg, Sotomayor, Breyer and Kagan to give them a five-member majority — and one of those was the decision regarding the citizenship question in the 2020 census.

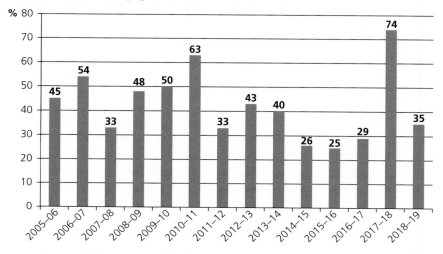

Figure 9.2 Frequency (%) of conservative victories in 5–4 decisions

Identical twins and odd couples

The two justices whose opinions most closely mirrored one another in this term were Clinton appointee Stephen Breyer and Obama appointee Elena Kagan (see Table 9.3). They both sit on the moderately liberal wing of the Court and would therefore not always be in step with their more strongly ideological fellow Democrat nominees, justices Ginsburg and Sotomayor — the identical twins of the previous term.

Table 9.3 Agreement and disagreement between justices, 2013–19

Term:	2013–14	2014–15	2015–16	2016–17	2017–18	2018–19
Two justices most in agreement	Thomas Alito	Breyer Ginsburg	Kennedy Kagan	Kennedy Kagan	Ginsburg Sotomayor	Breyer Kagan
Two justices most in disagreement	Alito Sotomayor	Thomas Sotomayor	Thomas Ginsburg	Thomas Ginsburg	Alito Sotomayor	Thomas Ginsburg/ Sotomayor

Different working styles

The nine justices of the Supreme Court are very different — in their ways of working as well as their judicial philosophy. Some work more quickly than others; some talk more than others. Figure 9.3 shows the very significant differences in the speed with which the nine justices write their opinions. Ruth Bader Ginsburg — by far the oldest member of the Court at 87 — is the quickest worker, taking an average of only 71 days to write her six majority opinions. At the other end of the scale, Bush appointee Samuel Alito took an average of 132 days to write his seven majority opinions.

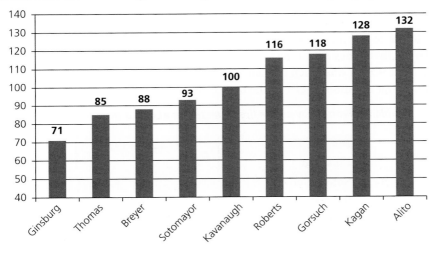

Figure 9.3 Days between oral argument and majority opinion

Table 9.4 shows the average number of questions each justice asked per oral argument. These figures show just how verbally busy these times of legal argument before the Court can be. Consider that Justice Sotomayor alone asked an average of 24 questions per oral argument! The two cases in this term which saw the

most questions fired from the bench were the gerrymandering case and the census question case — hardly surprising as they were both regarded as landmark decisions and both resulted in 5–4 decisions. These two cases engendered respectively 275 and 219 questions! (Oral argument typically lasts for 1 hour for each case.)

At the other end of the scale is Justice Clarence Thomas, who in March 2019 broke a 3-year period of silence in the courtroom by asking three questions during the *Flowers* v *Mississippi* oral argument. They were his only questions of the term.

One other point raised in Table 9.4 is the number of questions asked by the Court's newest member Brett Kavanaugh, who came third in the league table of the average number of questions asked per oral argument.

Table 9.4 Average number of questions per oral argument, 2018–19

Justice	Average
Sotomayor	24
Breyer	19
Kavanaugh	16
Kagan	15
Gorsuch	14
Roberts	13
Alito	13
Ginsburg	8
Thomas	0

As for asking the first question in each oral argument, this seems now to be the preserve of justices Ginsburg and Sotomayor — the two Clinton appointees. Between them, they asked the first question in 80% of oral arguments in this term (see Table 9.5). It was much the same in the previous term when they combined to ask the first question in 71% of the oral arguments.

Table 9.5 Frequency as the first questioner at oral argument, 2018–19

Justice	Frequency (%)
Ginsburg	41
Sotomayor	39
Roberts	13
Alito	7
Kagan	3
Breyer	1
Gorsuch	1
Thomas	0
Kavanaugh	0

What lessons can be learnt from this term?

So what lessons are there to be learnt from this first term of the Supreme Court with its present membership? Here are three.

Justice Kavanaugh was more centrist than expected in his first term

With the replacement of Justice Anthony Kennedy by Brett Kavanaugh, Republicans had hoped that with five reliable conservative votes on the Court — Thomas, Roberts, Alito, Gorsuch and Kavanaugh — this term, and subsequent ones, would see the conservative agenda sweeping all before it. As Adam Liptak wrote in the *New York Times* ('A Supreme Court term marked by shifting alliances and surprise votes', 29 June 2019), this Supreme Court term 'was expected to be a blood bath for its four-member liberal wing'. It wasn't. Kennedy's replacement by Kavanaugh was expected to shift the Court's centre of gravity to the right. It did. He certainly made some very unexpected alliances during his first term.

Table 9.6 Percentage of 5–4 decisions on which Justice Kavanaugh agreed with his colleagues

Justice	% agreed on 5–4 decisions
John Roberts	72
Samuel Alito	67
Stephen Breyer	49
Elena Kagan	44
Clarence Thomas	44
Sonia Sotomayor	40
Neil Gorsuch	40
Ruth Bader Ginsburg	36

As Table 9.6 shows, on the 5–4 decisions, Justice Kavanaugh agreed more frequently with Clinton appointee Stephen Breyer and Obama appointee Elena Kagan than with his fellow Trump appointee Neil Gorsuch, with whom he agreed in only 8 of the 20 5–4 decisions. Justice Kavanaugh was the person most frequently in the majority on divided cases — in 81% of them — followed by Chief Justice Roberts (73%) and Elena Kagan (71%). As Liptak commented: 'For now, at least, it is possible to make the case that Justice Kavanaugh is the new swing justice.'

The Court avoided certain cases to avoid further controversy

Following the bitter confirmation battle over Brett Kavanaugh's nomination to the Court, there seemed to be a determined effort by the Court to avoid further controversy — at least for this term. As a result, highly controversial cases on abortion and gay rights were not granted a hearing. But they are almost certain to appear in the not too distant future.

Some of the Court's significant work went below the radar

Although most of the Court's work time is spent hearing and deciding argued cases, from time to time the Court is asked to issue emergency applications — questions

that need a quick 'yes' or 'no' from the Court. Because these are not argued and announced in the conventional way, they do not appear in the end-of-term statistics that we analyse in this chapter. But in two such emergency applications during this term — one on a restrictive abortion law in Louisiana and another on President Trump's asylum policy — Chief Justice Roberts joined the Court's four liberals to block both. Maybe the Court is finally turning into the Roberts Court?

Comparison

The nature of the Supreme Court in the USA is rather different from that in the UK, which in turn means the decisions made and how they are viewed is often vastly different:

- While the UK Supreme Court does not decide all cases unanimously, it is far less divided than the US Supreme Court. This is evidenced in the 11–0 verdict in the case regarding the prorogation of Parliament, and indeed in the numerous other cases in which far fewer justices sit. In contrast, a 5–4 verdict is quite commonplace in the US Supreme Court.
- Justices in the USA are far simpler to categorise as 'conservative' or 'liberal', 'strict' or 'loose' constructionist than their UK counterparts. This is due in large part to the appointment process but also to the highly politicised nature of many of the cases that come to the US Supreme Court. The UK Supreme Court may be becoming more political in its rulings, but it lacks the power of the US Supreme Court in doing so.
- The US and UK Supreme Courts are increasingly similar in the way pressure groups try to use them to advance their own agenda. The UK Supreme Court has seen cases about abortion and LGBT rights supported by civil liberties groups and Christian groups in opposition to each other. The role of pressure groups is far more pronounced in the USA with groups bringing cases and submitting amicus curiae briefs. However, there is a growing similarity between the two countries.

Summary

In this chapter we have analysed the statistics of the 2018–19 Supreme Court term and found that:

- The nine justices were in the majority on 5–4 decisions a similar number of times each.
- The conservative wing of the Court was less dominant in this term than in the previous term.
- The justices have very different working styles in terms of the speed at which they write their majority opinions and the frequency with which they ask questions at oral argument.
- Justice Kavanaugh was more of a centrist in his first term than expected and less in agreement with his fellow Trump appointee Neil Gorsuch than expected.
- The Court tried hard to avoid controversy where it could.
- Chief Justice Roberts was found giving a five-member majority to both the conservative and the liberal quartets and in so doing might be regarded as the new swing justice to replace Justice Kennedy.